GW00759232

Soul and Reality

Metaphysics, Magic and Inner Search for a New Era of Awareness

ISBN 978-1-4709-0963-5

Contents

Introduction

This book explores:

- Spiritual Physics
- Esoteric Kabbalah
- Inner Alchemy
- Soul, death and reincarnation
- Ethics and approaches for renewed Awareness

The themes we are going to explore here are somewhat complex but I have tried to present them as clearly and succinctly as possible so that they are accessible to everyone and not just to experts in the field. My aim has been to make sense of the ideas rather than simply present the superficial facts and to offer readers my personal reflections in a context that is broad and well-versed on a cultural front.

This book, fruit of twenty years experience, is the 'state of the art' of my personal research; it describes paths and models in the light of the great changes to come and of the necessary awakening of consciousness that will characterize the imminent future of humanity.

My spiritual path began at an early age in a Catholic setting and then moved on towards Gnostic Christianity and Theosophy. It passed through the experience of Damanhurian community life, encountering various realities in the vast panorama of Italian and international New Age movements and later matured through personal research, (though not solitary or without moments of sharing and precious comparison). It was stimulated by a study of the neo-Gnostic and *Thelemic* ideas of Shamanism during a year spent in Africa and by the Sufism of the Middle East, which I explored during the five years I spent there for professional reasons. Since my return to Italy in 2009 my intention has been to focus on achieving a healthy and well-founded spiritual growth but also to promote discussion and cooperation between free thinkers who are interested in being the avant-garde of real renewal, not only in terms of *knowledge* but above all, of *living*: individuals who sense that the key to a conscious and authentic re-awakening lies in the values of personal liberty and responsible self-determination.

If in my last book *Nothing but Oneself* I attempted to describe my personal approach to spiritual research and 'frontier' investigations, and not without a certain amount of provocation, in this book I have concentrated on the most significant aspects of that research. I begin with a general overview based on past experience and conclude with some recent transpersonal and metaphysical elaborations, without neglecting to propose - in the epilogue – some further considerations.

These pages, having originated in my diaries, are inevitably based upon a wide-ranging examination of the subjects I have explored. But the information and reflections they contain do not pretend to be particularly exhaustive or in-depth for at least three of the following reasons:

1.   Firstly, I wish to remain consistent in my approach, at times supplying directions and hypotheses for working that allow the reader to actively apply him/herself to

examining aspects of personal interest more deeply and so obtain the most significant and efficient result.

2.   Secondly, because it is above all about subjective *feeling*, and the written word not only becomes a limited instrument in itself but also circumscribes the concepts and the sensitivity that it refers to. Therefore it is neither opportune nor possible to write a decisive book on the themes dealt with here, at least, unless one writes a historical-academic essay and that is something that I do not wish to do.

3.   And thirdly, because spiritual research is always and nevertheless *open* on infinite levels and the pretence of supplying definitive elements, or even just a close examination that discourages reflection or inner searching is not only restrictive but also misleading.

In the last chapter I describe the phases of my *working method* to furnish an example, to be perfected, of the path and its application in daily life. The meditation practices that I outline can be described and shared in real time in future meetings or specific seminars.

In the first appendix, I describe in more depth, the fundamental purpose, according to Esoteric Physics, for which our reality manifests itself.

Being a rather technical subject I decided to place it in an appendix so that the reader can choose whether or not to refer to it while reading or proceed more quickly, following the principal guiding themes and dedicate time to it at a later date.

In Appendix II, I have introduced an esoteric and metaphysical perspective of time, which will be the subject of successive argumentation. The subject of time (and eventual *time travel*) is a fascinating one and not new to ancient esoteric and shamanic traditions but it needs to be considered using logic of a more mature and complex nature than that of H.G. Wells' *Time Machine*.

I will also be providing further updates and in-depth analyses to my readers through conferences, specific seminars and by means of the Internet.

Carlo Dorofatti
(September 2010)

Metaphysical and Multi-dimensional Scenarios

Then there was not non-existent nor existent:
there was no realm of air, nor sky beyond it.
What covered in, and where? And what gave shelter?
was water there, unfathomed depth of water?

Death was not then, nor was there aught immortal:
no sign was there, the day's and night's divider.
That one thing, breathless, breathed by its own nature
apart from it was nothing whatsoever.

Darkness there was: at first concealed in darkness,
this All was indiscriminate chaos.
All that existed then was void and formless;
by the great power of warmth was born that unit.

Thereafter rose desire in the beginning,
Desire after the primal seed and germ of spirit.
Sages who searched with their heart's thought
discovered the existent's kinship in the non-existent.

Transversely was their severing line extended:
what was above it then, and what below it?
There were begetters, there were mighty forces,
Free action here and energy of yonder.

Who verily knows and who can here declare it,
whence it was born and whence comes this creation?
The gods are later than this world's production.
Who knows, then, whence it first came into being?

9

He the origin of this creation,
whether he formed it all or did not form it,
Whose eye controls this world in highest heaven,
He verily knows it, or perhaps he knows it not.

Rig Veda X.129 – The Song of Creation
(circa 3.900 a.C.)
Sanskrit translation: Friedrich Max Müller

The Birth of the World

The world is being born now. It is being born continuously. At this very moment, Consciousness creates its possible expressions: Evolution determines its manifestation. Depending on our level of Consciousness and Evolution we as beings participate in it more or less consciously.

The myths of every epoch and its peoples seem to agree that 'universes' are born in a primordial and transcendent nothingness from the *dreams* of an Absolute Consciousness as anomalous waves in the sea of All.

The Supreme Being can thus know itself and understand itself through the universes, just as our image is reflected in a mirror. Each universe is the expression of a new and different equilibrium: each one becomes, in its own way, a relative manifestation that is temporal and dynamic of the All.

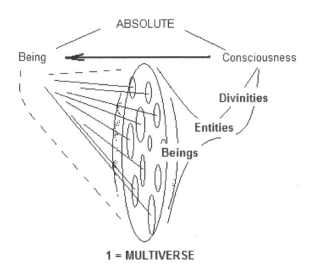

1 = MULTIVERSE

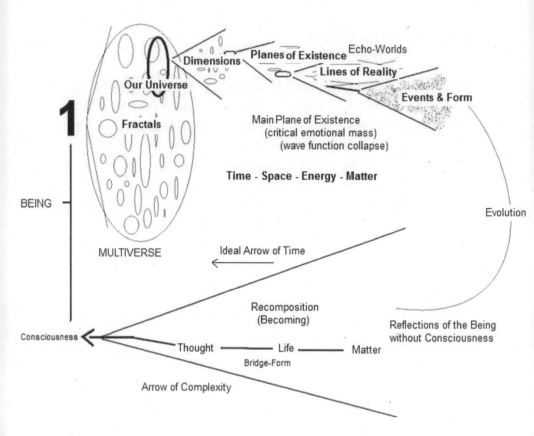

Together the universes comprise an infinite 'multi-versal' kaleidoscope. They are reflected in that which the Absolute Being acquires infinite Consciousness of Itself, even though it is immobile, generative, eternally omni-comprehensive and totally complete as such.

The Being nourishes itself. The primordial universes give 'substance' to the dreams of *God*, where every reality can exist. These same universes – each and every part – are generated by primordial energies which, in their turn, become archetypes and cosmic phenomena, laws, geometries and vital processes: the instruments through which Consciousness – in its turn distributed on diverse levels – evolves in every atom, in every cell, in every body and in every thought.

In extreme synthesis, interpreting esoteric tradition, these levels of consciousness are represented as primordial 'forces' laws and intelligent entities. They are the Eons, according to Gnostic Christian terminology, the *Neteru* of Egyptian myth or perhaps we might even call them, the 'Great Old Ones', to re-evoke the vertiginous visions of H.P. Lovecraft. They are the existential and conscious Archetypes (or pre-Archetypes) of our mind itself: the Primeval Divinities.

In order to exist, the possible expressions of reality have to expand the territory of their own awareness, with the aim of recognizing themselves and finally reconstructing themselves but above all, of *re-evolving* in the infinite in which they originate, through endless combinations of the possible.
It is as if – paradoxically – the Absolute is insatiable in renewing Consciousness of itself. And every time such Consciousness is dissolved into Nothingness to then create itself again, it renews itself: such dynamics are at once eternal and yet simultaneous, infinite and pulsating, between manifest and immanifest, noumenon and phenomenon, omniscience and exploration, eternity and becoming, order and chaos.

Our Universe, in its entirety, is none other than one of these systems of reality: an opportunity for renewed awareness. It is the crystal in which Consciousness splinters into fragments, little by little delineating possible geometries, to then reflect itself infinitely, to evolve and in the final analysis, play hide and seek with itself.

The Breath of Brahma

According to mythical images, Consciousness (or perhaps that *aspect* of Absolute Consciousness that we might include in the concept of 'Cosmic-Human Soul') expresses an act of will and creative love. It emanates, it is a *vibration* with the ability to generate *a wave of existence*: to manifest itself from this Cosmos in which laws and significance are progressively discovered. It will assume a shape and consistency that can be perceived and lived by consciousness, infused in the dimensions and bodies that will take on material Form, life, thoughts, entities and gods in the making.

We are all of this. Each one of us is an emanation of the Absolute Consciousness. Even though, paradoxically, we stop being so until we rediscover our primordial and eternal nature. This arrives through an understanding of renewed existential formulas or else through discovering the meaning of our life, the knowledge and experience of which must lead to the re-evolution of Cosmic Consciousness in time.

In Hindu metaphor this process is expressed as the *great breath of Brahma* which creates and destroys worlds in an incessant cyclical rhythm. God breathes out and the universe proceeds from the appearance of *laya*, or neutral centre, or else from the primordial meeting point of forces: the field of aggregation. With the intake of breath the universe is called back to the source and ceases to exist, but on the act of breathing out again manifestation begins anew.

Being *(Para-Brahman)* reveals itself in this field of forces, presented by Cosmic Consciousness in the form of *Human Consciousness*. Thus Being and Consciousness reveal and show themselves, they fragment and recompose: DISSOLVE and COAGULATE. COALESCE

14

In the ultimate analysis, what is *the voice of the Self* if not the boom of God's breath in our inner silence? The memory of the primordial Will?

29. For I am divided for love's sake, for the chance of union.
30. This is the creation of the world, that the pain of division is as nothing, and the joy of dissolution all.

Aiwass – Liber AL vel Legis, I

In Islamic tradition it is said: "I was a treasure unknown then I desired to be known so I created a Creation to which I made myself known, then they knew Me". The question of *being* and the soul has occupied eminent philosophers and thinkers from Parmenide to Eraclitus, from Socrates to Plato and Plotinus, resurfacing after centuries of 'darkness' in the Middle Ages with Cusanus, Erasmus of Rotterdam, Pico of Mirandola and Bacon of the Renaissance: a period in which the great Christian philosophers such as St. Augustine and St. Thomas Aquinas nevertheless managed to make their mark. And finally with the most recent illuminists – Hume, Leibniz, Kant, Fichte and Nietzsche – to arrive at a *peak* in the magic and *Thelemic-Hermetic* renaissance of the early years of last century. I personally like to single them out as a forewarning of scientific, cultural, social and political ferment.

Today all of this can be translated into the language of Physics. Think for example of the concept of the *holographic universe* (Bohm, Aspect, Pribram) which, in the 1980's, explained how the known material world is nothing more than the illusory multi-form projection of a single source.

To illustrate this point, below I include several excerpts from the famous article *Does Objective reality Exist, or is the Universe a Phantasm?* by Michael Talbot – Ref: https://www.dmt-nexus.me/forum/default.aspx?g=posts&t=4807

Bohm believes the reason subatomic particles are able to remain in contact with one another regardless of the distance separating them is not because they are sending some sort of mysterious signal back and forth but because their separateness is an illusion. He argues that at some deeper level of reality such particles are not individual entities but are actually extensions of the same fundamental something.

[...]

According to Bohm, the apparent faster-than –light connection between subatomic particles is really telling us that there is a deeper level of reality we are not privy to, a more complex dimension beyond our own. . [...]. And, he adds, we view objects such as subatomic particles as separate from one another because we are seeing only a portion of their reality. Such particles are not separate 'parts' but facets of a deeper and more underlying unity. [...] And since everything in physical reality is comprised of these 'eidolons', the universe is itself a projection, a hologram.

In addition to its phantom like nature, such a universe would possess rather startling features. If the apparent separateness of subatomic particles is illusory, it means that at a deeper level of reality all things in the universe are infinitely interconnected. The electrons in a carbon atom in the human brain are connected to the subatomic particles that comprise every salmon that swims, every heart that beats and every star that shimmers in the sky. Everything interpenetrates everything and although human nature may seek to categorize and pigeonhole and subdivide, the various phenomena of the universe, all apportionments are of necessity artificial and all of nature is ultimately a seamless web.

16

In a holographic universe even time and space could no longer be viewed as fundamentals. Because concepts such as location break down in a universe in which nothing is truly separate from anything else, time and three-dimensional space, (like the images of the fish on the TV monitors) would also have to be viewed as projections of this deeper order. At its deeper level reality is a sort of super hologram in which the past, present and future exist simultaneously. [...]

If a hologram of a rose is cut in half and then illuminated by a laser, each half will still be found to contain the entire image of the rose. Indeed even if the halves are divided again, each snippet of film will be found to contain a smaller but intact version of the original image. Unlike normal photographs every part of a hologram contains all the information possessed by the whole. The 'whole in every part' nature of a hologram provides us with an entirely new way of understanding organization and order.

[...]

everything in a grain of sand ~ William Blake

Allowing, for the sake of argument, that the super hologram is the matrix that has given birth to everything in our universe, at the very least it contains every subatomic particle that has been or will be – every configuration of matter and energy that is possible, from snowflakes to quasars, from blue whales to gamma rays. It must be seen as a sort of cosmic storehouse of 'All That Is'.

[...]

Such findings suggest that it is only in the holographic domain of consciousness that such frequencies are sorted out and divided up into conventional perceptions.

But the most mind-boggling aspect of Program's holographic model of the brain is what happens when it is put together with Boehm's theory. For if the concreteness of the world is but a secondary reality and what is 'there' is actually a holographic blur of frequencies and if the brain is also a hologram and only selects some of the frequencies of this blur and mathematically transforms them into sensory perceptions, what becomes of objective reality? Put quite simply, it ceases to exist. As the religions of the East have long upheld, the material world is Maya, an illusion, and although we may think we are physical beings moving through a physical world, this too is an illusion.

We are really 'receivers' floating through a kaleidoscopic sea of frequency and what we extract from this sea and transmogrify into physical reality is but one channel from many extracted out of the super hologram

This striking new picture of reality, the synthesis of Bohm and Pribram's views, has come to be called the-holographic-paradigm and although many scientists have greeted it with scepticism, it has galvanized others. A small but growing group of researchers believe it may be the most accurate model of reality science has arrived at thus far. [...]

In a universe in which individual brains are actually indivisible portions of the greater hologram and everything is infinitely interconnected, telepathy may merely be the accessing of the holographic level.

[...]

The holographic paradigm also has implications for so-called hard sciences like biology. Keith Floyd, a psychologist at Virginia Intermont College, has pointed out that if the concreteness of reality is but a holographic illusion, it would no longer be true to say the brain produces consciousness. Rather it is consciousness that creates the appearance of the brain — as well as the body and everything around us we interpret as physical.

Such a turnabout in the way we view biological structures has caused researchers to point out that medicine and our under standing of the healing process could also be transformed by the holographic paradigm. If the apparent physical structure of the body is but a holographic projection of consciousness, it becomes clear that each of us is much more responsible for our

Bruce Lipton   18

health than current medical wisdom allows. What we now view as miraculous remissions of disease may actually be due to changes in consciousness which in turn effect changes in the ⃒ *hologram of the body.*

Similarly, controversial new healing techniques such as visualization may work so well because in the holographic domain of thought, images are ultimately as real as 'reality'. [...]

What we perceive as reality is only a canvas waiting for us to draw upon it any picture we want. [...]

Perhaps we agree on what is 'there' or 'not there' because what we call consensus reality is formulated and ratified at the level of the human unconscious at which all minds are infinitely interconnected.

The Creation of the Material Worlds

It happened, when this our Great inversion took place, from the essence of all nothingness to finity extended in innumerable categories, that an incalculably vast system was produced. Merely by chance, chance in the truest sense of the term, we are found with gods, men, stars, planets, devils, colours, forces and all the materials of the Cosmos: and with time, space and causality, the conditions limiting and involving them all.

Aleister Crowley[1], BERASHITH - 1902

---

[1] In the course of the book I will be quoting from Aleister Crowley – just as I will refer to Theosophy, Gurdjieff,
Aurobindo, Krishnamurti, Osho and many others. However, every time Crowley is mentioned there are those who are immediately scandalized. They are undoubtedly ill-prepared on the subject and have been mislead by the amount of nonsense in circulation regarding a figure who, though

According to esoteric, kabbalistic and alchemical cosmogenesis – but in many ways, also in terms of modern physics - the material world (energy/mass) is not immediately generated as an effect of the clash between primeval forces (*primeval laws*), rather its creation, considered from the point of view of the human being, follows a series of passages: the process of creation happens in non-time, however, in order to understand this idea we need to make use of logical sequences in order to describe it.

Our Universe is above all a concept:

- Manifold
- Diversified
- Dynamic

Concepts that are translated into a temporal, dimensional and spatial universe.
At the beginning reality is *virtual* and not yet translated into matter-life-perception-experience. Its *existence* is only potential: at the act of creation we are still in the field of inexistent Being, in the *World of Ideas*.

---

certainly controversial, willingly and unwillingly, is worth discovering and considering. I would like to reassure readers that despite his audacious experimentation at the height of the Victorian era; his anarchistic and provocative looks and a certain extravagance that could render him strangely unpleasant – Crowley was not the founder of Satanism, even though he was anti-clerical. And he never sacrificed or ate children. That said, I do not think that Crowley needs me to defend him and as for the rest I am not willing to take it on board. However, I do acknowledge the breadth of his work in setting out the theory and practice of a magic–realization of the Self in the light of new existential and spiritual paradigms. He was without doubt among its precursors when the Age of Aquarius or the New Era had yet to be talked about.

The inexistent is the field that renders true that which is existent and real, through 'existential significance' attributing significance to things, life, emotions and thought.

The Absolute is Nothingness and the All.
Nothingness is the All without Consciousness.
The All is Nothingness full of Consciousness.

The creation processes happen outside of creation itself, therefore outside of time. They generate a field that is already the expression of Being but 'inexistent'. In that state the universe is inexistent because we cannot perceive it, try it out, or give it significance: to do those things we need relationship, or *growth*. We need time/space, that is, a *filter* which is able to distinguish and scan reality and the evolved interaction between diversity.

In order to do this we use the *mind*. The mind is strictly correlated to the phenomena of time and space: It is the instrument for scanning and fixing. Everything comes down to the mind and eventually we have to act to evade it, in order to travel in or manipulate time and space, but that is another story...

The World of Ideas – or the *Macrocosmic Mind* – is the chaotic and virtual container of all times and of all manifestations and possible existential directions, without any of them being defined: it is the *eternal present*, the 'sphere of Time' where everything is, but does not exist. It corresponds to the kabbalistic *Ain-Soph*, the *Thelemic*[2] body of *Nuit*, which defines the universal field of the possible and keeps it unified.

Now, we can but try to make an interpretative synthesis of the various cosmogeneses, handed down to us through the images of myth and those of Western and Eastern religions.

In order for material Form to manifest a direction *in* time is needed, or the possibility of a relationship with multiplicity, space and perception.

In the world of ideas, or in the *concept* of a universe created by a vibrational wave from Absolute Consciousness, absolute nothingness (a potential but non-existent universe) enters into relationship with absolute time (the container of all 'existent' possibilities) emitting an infinitely creative energy, that will orient itself according to a new geometry of laws from which dimensions and existential levels will ensue: the creation.

The Egyptians assigned this role to the Creator God, who was not Ra, in as much as he was absolute Consciousness and all encompassing, but Ptah, the Demiurge God. Today modern

---

[2] With this adjective I am referring to the concepts and experiences that inspire the research themes and magic-mystical practice recovered and brought to life by Aleister Crowley in the early years of the last century. The Thelemic path (from Thelema, which in Greek means Will) better known as Current 93 (the number, according to the Greek Kabbalah that is associated both with the word Will and Love, thus establishing a link between the two principles), has been further developed by successive Initiate Orders which when not deviate or contaminated, form a bridge between esoteric traditions and the avant-garde of esoteric research at the dawn of this New Era. As far as I am concerned the Thelemic path has become the most 'up to date' body of doctrine and knowledge and the principle technical reference for those who, always maintaining the necessary caution, wish to approach Magic in its many forms.

science is investigating all of this in mathematical terms, both theoretically and experimentally.

We try to interpret these processes moment by moment, not outside but *inside ourselves* in relation to reality and its 'keys of access'. Because it is inside of us, in the depths of our divine essence that all of this is continuously carried out. According to esoteric thought, it is we, who are the representative particles of this same Consciousness and Cosmic Energy: the creators of *all-that-is-and-ever-will be.*

According to *Esoteric Physics*, the process of creating worlds, galaxies and all existing things - all that will become life and evolution – passes through what we would traditionally define as the *world of numbers*: a space-time or 'vibrational' sieve. In this case we are not talking about the concept of *numbers* as we think of them mathematically but as numerical relationships rather than single entities. The 'world of numbers' is precisely a dimension in itself, the link between the world of ideas (unitary) and the potential world of the material (manifold). *The world of numbers* and the pattern of relationships that define the measurements of so called 'sacred geometry' is therefore the matrix of the manifest world. The same mechanism that geometrically identifies the material world and its objects, we find reflected in the systems that codify life and its possible evolutionary directions: DNA, is our 'antenna' for tuning in on reality.

Human Consciousness – which in fact is not yet 'human' until it has truly *realized* the experience of 'humanity' – has to conduct its evolution inside this universal scheme: it reflects itself or better still, it instils itself into the material world of Form to trigger a process of self-awareness, that contemporaneously renders every thing 'true' by making it 'exist' in absolute terms.

With this in mind, it is perhaps useful to re-elaborate the modern myth of 'ascension': it is not we who have to 'ascend' to the fifth dimension or wherever (if it is, it has always been, *here and now* and is therefore 'our home') but it is the fifth dimension (it is God!) that wants to apply itself to this possible existence: and we are the vehicle! In fact: we are IT.

The Concept of Reality

Therefore I offer you my contemplations on the infinite universe and the innumerable worlds.

Giordano Bruno

The entire creative process happens instantaneously, simultaneously and continuously. There is no beginning but rather a combination of *states* and *intensity* of Being diversely modulated and invigorated by phenomena operating on the reference plane of existence.

Inside every tiny particle of conceivable matter this process renews itself continuously. The creative energy emits directions and planes with different densities and variables and yet every thing is connected with the All, and every one of its smallest constituent parts contains the infinite.

Time

Just as with space and the things and beings that surround us, time is also the fruit of an illusion of the mind: time itself is part of the great experiential theatre created for the evolutionary goals of Consciousness.

Time is in its own way a manifestation of primordial Energy, of the All. For us it becomes the indispensable instrument through which we express and read our perceptive experiences – which have descended into this manifestation – and therefore through which we give significance to this form of existence: to events to life, to 'history'.
But if we separate from our material nature, we can emancipate ourselves from our limits in space and time and interact with reality outside of the limits of the cause and effect established by our current mind: we can access a superior level of relationship with reality, with power over illusion and synchronicity. Or, at least, remind ourselves that our reality is nothing more than a theatrical representation and, by going behind the scenes every now and again we can 'return home'.

On a technical plane, 'time' more than anything else is the 'container of possibilities': an immense *circular sphere of the eternal present*. There is no flow; everything is there, to design a complex geography of potential events. It is a multi-dimensional field curved in on itself, just like space. The universe is in itself non-local, or indistinct, contemporaneous and simultaneous: The One.
Nevertheless, within the confines of the universal field, time, expressed and perceived in a chronological sense, is important and indispensable: it serves to measure growth, to give a sense of reading (and therefore a sense of consciousness) to the

transformation of events or the material world of Form at every level.

For further elements on the concept of time from an Esoteric Physics point of view please consult Appendix II.

Levels of Reality

To explore 'reality' we have to begin from the supposition that what our current senses perceive is nothing more than *one* of its possible aspects, or a manifestation consistent with our perceptive and elaborative possibilities. We are talking about a kind of meditation (or better still many levels of meditation) and consequently of a meeting point between the Absolute, higher levels of reality, the mind and the biological senses that limit our experience.

Everything that we participate in is 'just' our plane of existence, or the current reality:

- Three-dimensional
- Human
- Terrestrial
- Consensual

Our plane of existence is the result of a sensorial circuit of a consensual and conventional kind; therefore, it is all relative. It is the result of the meeting between *all that is* and that which can be differentiated and perceived through the exercise of our current senses. They in their turn are developing so that a possible level of consciousness can interpret this existence and attribute ever more complex significance to it, transcending and identifying it as an aspect of the Absolute. It is thus transformed from *mechanics* (field of laws) to *awareness* (field of choice), or from a precarious and unstable manifestation to an incorruptible presence, from the chaotic illusions of the senses to an aware experience of consciousness.

Our reality is - to all intents and purposes - a bubble of appearances: and we have the task (the challenge?) of making it real and everlasting in the Absolute by means of ourselves.

The thoughts - and the considerations that follow - need to be seen in the context of spiritual, alchemical and magical disciplines and therefore with 'another' kind of sensitivity – or perhaps with a more authentic sensitivity that we have yet to reawaken – rather than be investigated with the rational mind. We need to use *the breath of the thinking heart*, as I like to call it: try to read, understand and absorb these ideas with your body, your heart and not just with your brain.

Use the breath. Feel the correspondence and the call of truth inside yourself. But be careful: we are not talking about expedients. It is necessary to use all your experience to comprehend, so that reading and study becomes a real meditation practice, a kind of yoga-study. Learning to use other parts of yourself to navigate with a new and different logic helps to break away from the ordinary rhythm of the mind. It is necessary to change perspective and comprehend new stimuli on many levels; otherwise there is no point in proceeding. These themes are meditation practices and not just ideas to store in your head.

For example, in the practice of *Jnana Yoga* (the *path of knowledge*) the liberation (Moksha) and therefore the union with God can be acquired for half the *knowledge of Brahman*, recognizing Brahman as your own Self. The liberation from Samsāra (the cycle of birth and death) is achieved thanks to the realization of the identity of the individual soul (*Jīva*) in the Supreme Soul.

This mainstay of Vedanta philosophy considers metaphysical ignorance (*Avidya*) the cause of all human suffering and attachment to the material world: it acts like a veil (*Maya)* preventing Jīva from perceiving her real and divine nature. In its smallness and ignorance the individual soul convinces itself that it is separate and different from Brahman. The knowledge of Brahman (*or Brahma Jnana*) removes this veil allowing Jīva to re-establish herself in her own essential nature: *Sat-Chit-Ananda* (Existence, Knowledge, Beatitude).

Our Reality

Our plane of existence appears solid and three-dimensional because we perceive things are solid to the touch and that time has a certain speed, which we measure in proportion to our perception of celestial dynamics.
These parameters determine the world of space-time-mass-energy that physics, astronomy, chemistry, the natural sciences and mathematics wish to interpret and exploit.

Inside a plane of reality or the reality that is commonly accepted as such, every individual develops their own *personal dimension*. Opinions and subjective meanings make up the *individual 'quasi-real'* (almost real), as defined by Theosophy.
The investigation of subjective dimensions is the concern of the human sciences, of psychology, sociology, and the arts and it is there, that mental and emotional dynamics, more than the perceptions of the senses, determine *what is real.*

Each one of us, beginning from our own quasi-real and our capacity to give significance to things can construct a bridge which reunites human experience to the All.

Let's look at it in more depth and examine what lies 'beyond' our subjective representation of reality and beyond the conventional plane of our material, human and earthly existence.

Beyond the veil of the quasi-real and the consensual suggestion that delineates the borders of our plane of existence (or our physical three-dimensional reality), we find a more complex 'supporting structure' that constitutes a much broader dimensional reality.

This wider level of reality or rather the combination of the band of frequencies in which our specific frequency is to be found, constitutes our *dimension* (our plane of existence), along with other possible frequencies or lines of reality that are dimensionally compatible with one another.
This dimension is our 'world', one of the numerous possible parallel worlds to be found among numerous dimensions and bands of possible frequencies.

'Our world', therefore, is a dimension which exists inside our current plane of existence but which belongs to a much wider possibility of *lines of reality* that are nevertheless part of the same 'dimension'.
The *universe of material Form*

as a whole consists of our world united to many other worlds-dimensions, defined as 'parallel worlds'. They are also described as such in the models of the universe explored by mathematics and physics.

The multi-world theory is not new; the first to introduce it was Hugh Everett in 1957. There are worlds, multiple worlds in our universe and each one develops on the basis of the dynamics derived from primeval energies and forces. For this reason we define and codify them as *derivative laws*. I use the term 'laws' even though it would be more appropriate to call them 'phenomena': the world is not made of 'laws' but of phenomena and we tend to codify them on the basis of our ability to interpret reality.

These same *derivative laws*, that we can imagine ruling our universe, become something even more specific at a dimensional level: In every world-dimension the fundamental laws correspond to a specific version of themselves and then by specializing on each plane of reality they become the 'physical laws' that we know of as gravity, electromagnetism and nuclear forces etc.

We can see that as we slowly *descend into the material world* the same dynamics are repeated but on different levels and scales. It begins with the primeval laws at the level of the 'multi-verses'; from there universal functions (derivative laws), are generated that function inside every specific universe. In the possible dimensions of our universe the derivative laws apply themselves to time, or better *in* time, seen as a flow from the past to the future and are known as 'time' (or temporal) matrices.

These matrices, which are different in every dimension, finally become the physical laws of each plane of existence, or the reality that is perceived at our current psycho-biological level.

30

The sequence is therefore as follows:

Structure	Functions	Level of Consciousness
Absolute (That-Which-Is-Real)	The Being / Consciousness of the Being	Being
Universes in the Absolute	Primeval Laws	Consciousness
Universe among Universes	Derivative Laws	Cosmic Soul
Parallel World of our Universe	Time Matrices	Cosmic Humanity
Our World/Dimension	Our Time Matrices	Dimensional Humanity
Lines of Reality	Physical Laws	Potential Living Humanity
Our Plain of Existence (3d)	Our Natural Physical Laws	Current Living Humanity
Individual Quasi-Real	Mental Dynamics	Current Individuality

The 'parallel worlds' – just as all possible states of being – are not 'from somewhere else' but, vibrating on different *frequencies*, they are all contemporary and interpenetrate.

In every temporally oriented world the *derivative laws* combine in a different way. Just as the respective time matrixes that operate on the dimensions are different, so too are the 'physical' laws that operate on each specific plane of existence.

Let's look at the diagram which begins from the individual 'quasi-real' and slowly rises.

1. Subjective reality is the plane of existence filtered by the individual quasi-real
2. The plane of existence is a dimensional world filtered by the senses of a species (consensual reality)
3. A dimensional world (or parallel world) is the result of the Universe filtered by time matrices (or, alternatively by the senses of more complex entities)
4. The Universe as a whole is the *multi-verse* filtered by derivative laws (or by the senses of higher entities) and

31

the final one is the 'REAL' filtered by primeval laws (or by the senses of higher 'Consciousnesses')

5. In the end (everywhere and always) we have the REAL, the Absolute; unmediated Being.

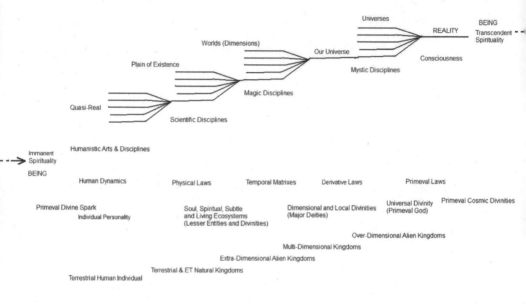

To sum up: the existent is not traceable in different 'places', but through the analysis and the differentiation of 'filters' and 'vibrations'. The REAL, everything, is here. Now, at this moment.

Our physical senses serve to *define* the reality that surrounds us, or better still our field of possible experiences. They are calibrated in such a way as to *filter* our field of reality.

They are not used therefore to perceive but rather to limit perceivable reality which is then processed by our respective conscious and mental patterns.

Aldous Huxley, in his *Doors of Perception* offers us a very interesting view of this idea:

According to such a theory[3], each one of us is potentially Mind at Large. But in so far as we are animals, our business is at all costs to survive. To make biological survival possible, Mind at Large has to be funnelled through the reducing valve of the brain and the nervous system. What comes out at the other end is a measly trickle of the kind of consciousness which will help us stay alive on the surface of this Particular planet.

Our specific plane *of existence* is therefore determined by two main filters: the senses and the personal mind. However, in this historical-evolutionary moment, we find ourselves in a condition of severe *handicap*, which does not allow us to truly live the reality that should be our 'province'.

Our incarnation ought to correspond to a level of reality– and therefore be *structured* by our vehicle of consciousness – that is much higher than that currently found on this planet, in this line of material reality.

---

[3] A reference to a theory of Bergson according to which 'The function of the brain, the nervous system and the organs of the senses are principally eliminatory and not productive'.

The Absolute Being and Us

Being is infinitely transcendent and immanent: it is 'beyond' but it is also 'every' thing and 'in every' thing at every level (universe, planet or microbe). Recognizing the All in every single part is a question of awareness since the Absolute Being is always and everywhere.

We are now living in a *perceptive convention*, of space, matter, the past and the future. The priority of perception in respect to the phenomenon itself leads to the perceptive nature of that said reality, thus the phenomena of physics (but also that which we call 'memory' and 'history') are only real in proportion to our ability (and willingness) to conceive of them.

It is we ourselves – each one of us – that defines the frontiers and therefore the limits of reality or the line of reality that we decide to access. It is we who decide to activate what is 'true' with its laws and mechanisms, its past and future!

It is we who, here, right now, moment by moment, regardless of whether we are conscious of it or not, establish the sequence in which we stand, our subjective reality of reference: the pertinent quasi-real. It is we who establish in which suggestion of reality we live, individually and therefore collectively.

Consequently we establish what is true and what is not, what has been and what will be, along with all the mechanisms of reality that we want to reveal and the laws that we want to function. We set out what can exist and what cannot, what we want to discover and what cannot be discovered; in the present or in the past.

Can we heal with our vital energy? Perhaps yes, if we decide that it is so; or absolutely not, if we do not want to open up that line of possibility. Did Atlantis exist? Perhaps it did if we want to access a certain line of reality and then we find its archaeological remains; or not: and we do not find anything. Or for someone else Atlantis still exists. The mechanism is for the most part consensual but the nearer we get to the centre of our real identity the more this *process of determining the truth* becomes localized and personal. Someone sees and someone else does not, someone can and someone else cannot: and both are right! And perhaps the year 2012 – give or take a year – will be a watershed for different levels of humanity and reality. But no one will notice the change, each person having constructed their own level of subjective reality.

The real does not have a structure of its own that is distorted by our mental interpretations: all of our being has to agree on the determination of ideal reality; it has to be in tune with that part of ourselves and our faculties that we are unaware of and that lie latent.

If we do not move our barycentre towards our real identity, we are subject to the reality of our mind rather than the determiners of it: the reality of the mind which, if we are unable to do anything else, invents the stage, play and characters of a drama without purpose.

It is important to bear in mind that when we observe our universe 'from the inside' we can interpret each phenomenon only and exclusively in relation to how much it is part of our awareness and with the means and senses at our disposal.
Reality is much richer and more eloquent than we are used to settling for, just as our nature is more expansive and expressive. Material Form and its continued transformation as we perceive it in time (cause and effect) is nothing more than the three-dimensional reflection of the *fractals* of a complex interaction of phenomena, energies and forces operating in an extremely vast multi-polar and multi-dimensional universe.

God savours Himself. In the act of savouring himself, He savours all creatures, not because they are creatures but because they are God. God creates this entire world absolutely in this instant.

Meister Eckhart

The *Threshold* or the Beyond

The extension of the self towards Awareness passes through an intermediate dimension between material Form and the Real that we can define as the 'Threshold', the Beyond or if we prefer the 'Other Side'. When we dream or travel on the astral planes or carry out explorations on the *frontier*, as in 'between one life and another', we find ourselves in this *Half-way World*. Just as entry into the material world of Form passes through the world of numbers, the way out passes through the Threshold: in the first case realty fragments, in the second it reassembles.

We can imagine the Threshold as:

- Beyond our material world
- As an interregnum between parallel worlds
- Between the universe of Form and the Real.

We are talking about a hyperspace in which disincarnate souls arrive and withdraw: it is not 'somewhere else' but rather the extended projection of a growing being.

Our incarnate physical body is therefore only a dimensional fraction of the greater reality that constitutes the complex soul/body.

Following the logic of reincarnation, we can say that the Threshold hosts the passage of those *packets of experiences* known as Souls which, by means of one incarnation after another ideally complete themselves.

F = Form (Universe - Body - Any Object)

T = Threshold (Subtle Worlds - Soul - Aura)

R = Real (Spirit - Being - Essence)

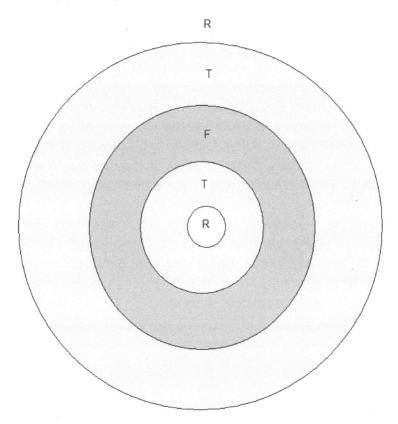

The sequence is usually thought of as: The Material World -The Other Side – The Absolute, or as Form-Threshold-Real.

Nevertheless everything is also reflected inside each and every thing: so let's not limit ourselves to the representation of transcendent directions, but complete it with that of the - perhaps more significant - immanent.

The Real is therefore that which is *beyond* but also *inside*.

Take a look at these illustrations of levels of reality – created at different times using different logic and a diagram taken from the book *No Boundary* by Ken Wilber that I warmly recommend you to read.

My diagram represents reality 'from high to low'; however the two extremes touch each other, without solutions of continuity. The most reduced level of reality is relative or individual (quasi-real), it is the point of departure on the scale of significance that continuously extending, leads to the Absolute. A reality in which through every single thing – on the various scales of interaction/perception/consciousness – one rediscovers the All.

We have to remember that the All is not 'somewhere else' in respect to where we find ourselves. Everything is *Here* and *Now*. It is necessary to acquire a new level of Consciousness to recognize and participate in the All through every idea and thing no matter how small or simple.

PERCEPTION	Extra-Dimensional Projection	Level of Reality
CONSCIOUSNESS	**'GOD'**	**BEING = ABSOLUTE REAL**
METAMORPHOSIS	**Primeval Deities**	MULTIVERSE
Theurgy		
	'Veil of the Abyss'	
ENLIGHTENMENT	**UNIVERSAL**	**OUR UNIVERSE**
Magic	**DIVINITY**	
Esoteric Physics		MOTHER WORLDS
Alchemy	**Deities**	
PARTIAL ILLUMINATION		PARALLEL WORLDS
	'Veil of the Senses'	
INTUITION		**OUR WORLD**
	Spiritual & Subtle Ecosystems	
Esotericism		
Quantum Physics		Existing Form growing on a plane of existence
ILLUSION / 'MAYA'	Natural Kingdoms	among different potential echo-worlds
Sensorial Perception Boundary	RACE-MIND	**CONSENSUAL REALITY**
Physics - Chemistry - Biology...	Human Ecosystems	Space-Time-Energy-Matter
ILLUSIONARY IDENTITY	Individual Souls	INDIVIDUAL QUASI-REAL
Psychology - Sociology...		
	'Veil of Immanence'	
ART & SPIRITUALITY	**INNER GOD**	**MEANINGS**

Spiritual Ecosystem	LEVELS OF REALITY	Awareness

Spiritual Ecosystem	LEVELS OF REALITY	Awareness
GOD Undefined Consciousness of the Being	**ABSOLUTE BEING** *THE REAL*	**CONSCIOUSNESS** Awakening
GRAIL - MYSTERIES	Primeval Laws	**Metamorphosis**
PRIMEVAL DEITIES	**UNIVERSES**	High Magic
abyss	Fields of Derivative Laws	**abyss**
Humankind Primeval Divinity	Derivative Laws Meeting Point **Universe of Forms** World of Ideas into the temporal chaotic sphere	**Enlightenment** Harmonization of the 'personalities' Magic Esoteric Physics
'Shattering of the Mirror'	World of Numbers	Alchemy
Major Divinities Ecosystem	**Parallel Worlds** Combined Derivative Laws (temporal matices)	**Partial Illumination** Awareness of our own soul structure
Temporal Ecosystem		
first veil		*first veil*
Local Deities **Spiritual Ecosystem**	**OUR WORLD** Existing Form growing on a PLANE OF EXISTENCE among different virtual Echo-Worlds	**Initiation** Interdisciplinary Knowledge (Gnosis)
Subtle Ecosystems		**Illusion - Maya** Sensorial Perception Limit
Natural Kingdoms (mineral, vegetable, animal)		Math - Physics Chemistry - Biology Natural Sciences
RACE-MIND Human Ecosystems	Space-Time Matter-Energy = CONSENSUAL REALITY	Philosophy Sociology - Anthropology Psychology
Individual Souls	Individual **Quasi-Real**	**Illusionary Identity**
Veil of Immanence **INNER GOD**	**MEANINGS**	**ART & SPIRITUALTY**

40

This diagram illustrates the development of reality according to three fundamental references: Being as the Subject, the Real as environment (object) and Consciousness intended as perception, knowledge and awareness applied to the various levels of possible reality. It is important to note that the distinction between Being, Real and Consciousness assumes a formal and non-substantial role.

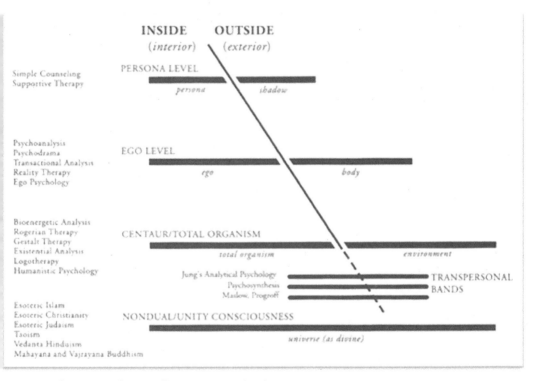

(Courtesy of Ken Wilber – No Boundary)

41

Behind the 'Scenes': Entities and Aliens

The Spirits of the Goetia are portions of the human brain.

Aleister Crowley

We conventionally call 'psycho-creatures' all those intelligences that, following a certain *esoteric* terminology, distinguish themselves as:

- Divinities
- Egregors
- Guardians, angels and angelicity
- Demons
- Energized thought forms and subtle creatures (or extra-dimensional beings that manifest in the same manner)
- Disincarnate presences and *helpers*
- Planetary spirits, elementals and those of nature
- Larvae and 'shells' or *phantoms*.

All these entities make up a complex multi-dimensional and spiritual ecosystem, as well as the energy food chain in which we are immersed and participate regardless of whether we are aware of it or not.

In general terms we can say that each one of these:

- Originates from a human aspect or from a personal a/o collective human projection
- Represents more or less active and intelligent 'information'

42

- Superimposes itself or presides over an energetic/physical field, influencing its dynamics at various levels
- Nourishes itself on vital a/o psychic a/o spiritual energy
- Can enter into communication with the human being for different reasons and in different ways
- Its manifestation can determine itself or be determined with great holographic versatility, influenced by the thought and suggestions that are applied to it.

Every psycho-creature contains and manages forces of a lower level, directing events in order to safeguard the *territory* from which it receives the energetic nourishment used for its own maintenance and development. The most complex entities 'know' how to cultivate their own resources by creating a suitable spiritual and subtle *habitat,* more or less in symbiosis with the human being and its evolution. The entities of a lower level often create a parasitic relationship with the energies or Form with which they enter into contact.

The human being is part of this spiritual eco-system and, as a *bridge-Form*, should be its evolved interpreter in relation to the material world.

If we are living in an eco-system, it is normal that beings from many other dimensions enter into contact with us or even make 'use' of us. According to esoteric tradition, extra a/o multi-dimensional Forms exist and continuously interact with us even though we do not realize it.

Perhaps in a previous phase of evolutionary human immaturity these entities – of different orders and degree – might have eventually constituted a scale of values towards the Real and Consciousness. Today, however, the psychic, astral, subtle or divine planes, as we often call them, are populated by entities that have absolved themselves of their function and now cloud and distance the human being from his essence and the reality of things, be they devils, spirits, angels or 'God'.

The time is right. We need to proceed with a change in consciousness, to purify, liberate and acknowledge that which lies in each one of us: our most profound Essence.

Incidentally, from this point of view ufological phenomenon and contactism can be considered part of a much wider scenario of the esoteric sciences or of those disciplines that study the link between our inner and outer worlds. There is no real demarcation between our consciousness and the object perceived by it. In the evaluation of UFO phenomena, extraterrestrials and aliens, and certainly before we push ourselves to classify races and draw conclusions as to their 'agendas', we have to establish if these entities are connected to 'alternative realities'.

The ufologist and classic contactee do not usually concern themselves with this.
Even less so the *abductee*[4], with good reason, if acting on good faith with interpretations of phenomena (because here we are

---

[4] 'Abductions' (or close encounters of the fourth kind, according to the classification of the astrophysicist Allen
Hynek), the presumed kidnappings of human beings by alien entities, represent one of the most interesting and controversial aspects of the ufological phenomena. The problem was brought to the attention of researchers at the beginning of the 1960's when the American academic John Fuller published a book *The Interrupted Journey* on the now famous experience of the married couple Barney and Betty Hill. They were placed under regressive hypnosis by the noted Boston psychiatrist Benjamin Simon and re-evoked a kidnapping episode on the part of small humanoids who,

only talking about interpretations) that insist on terrifying scenarios. They exclude – perhaps because they do not know – keys to reading that take into account vaster perspectives. For example the disciplines of trans-humanistic psychology, esoteric physics, the anthropology of the sacred and in the final analysis, reality and consciousness.

The UFO phenomenon seems to interact with the collective psyche and if the collective psyche 'takes on' certain forms, it might well take on those forms that make themselves available. If at a collective level we were to modify such a paradigm, we could verify if such phenomena assume different connotations just as physics theorizes on how phenomena behave according to the conditions of observation.

UFOs – the genuine manifestations – appear when they find the right *psychic contents* that will give shape to them, including solid form.
I know that it seems simplistic to reduce them to manifestations of consciousness but in the current context it helps if we consider other mechanisms from a higher level of observation.

For now, though, let's limit ourselves and begin with the idea that we are talking about a *Form* which is given *energy* that is part of an aspect of reality we have yet to discover.

The UFO phenomena represents a window on the beyond and also encourages us to investigate just how much is alien inside of us or at least to recognize how tightly we are bound to what we have been taught to believe the world is all about.

---

having led them on board a flying saucer, subjected them to a series of medical examinations.

Adopting a dualistic scheme (good-evil), reality assumes those self-same connotations. The forces of evil perceived as real and hostile and perhaps also materialized through UFO phenomena, could in reality be entities generated and nourished by us. They could be an *effect* of human behaviour that has lasted for millennia and not the historical cause of our status[5].

The awakening has to begin from *inside* of us. It is we who lend ourselves to games of illusion, deceit and pillage. There are many political, social, religious and cultural realities that tend to perpetuate what is a mechanism of energetic 'vampirism'. This is certainly one of the causes of Evil and it has been generated by Mankind itself. Continuing to perceive reality in terms of a good-evil dualism results in modifying the structure of what is real. We are capable of creating all the hells and paradises that we want. If we leave behind the idea of sin, the devil, the messiah and the enemy or the sheep-shepherd-wolf paradigm and the need to be continually reassured and saved (concepts of the Judaic-Christian matrix that have distorted the values of the *New Age* itself), the phenomenon would probably *change*

A metaphysical hypothesis with regard to the UFO phenomenon has already been explored by Carl G. Jung. In fact the pioneer of psychology often concerned himself with the UFO phenomenon in his writings and in particular in his celebrated essay *A Modern Myth: the things that one sees in the sky*, interpreting them as unconscious psychic representations linked to collectively relevant events.

---

[5] We should perhaps ask ourselves if abduction phenomena (with their many testimonials, memories emerging under hypnosis and implants) are not in their turn a deceptive cover up – or the opportunity seized and exploited to a fine art to conceal experimentation and military strategies which are tragically terrestrial!

After Jung, the scientist Jacques Vallée, who worked as an astronomer and collaborator with NASA in the 1970's took up the theme again but was fiercely opposed by the international ufological community. Its researchers were relentless in their desire to give the phenomenon – be it physical or psychic – a connotation of an interference that is somewhat 'other' in respect to our reality, preferring to place it on the physical rather than *para-physical* plane.

Nevertheless, in that same period, psychedelic experiences – the main interest of neuro-physicians, anthropologists, botanists and a plethora of 'flower children' (the roles often coincided!) - later brought to the attention of a wider public by Carlos Casteneda[6], seem to give serious credit to a far from simple interpretation of the question.

We should also not exclude the effect on reality a/o the psyche provoked by experiments with time and holographic technology, whether they be of this world or another.

Terence McKenna, in *True Hallucinations*, affirms with great optimism that: «... The UFO is a reflection of a future event that promises humanity's eventual mastery over time, space and

---

[6] See also the accounts of Terence McKenna and the more recent studies of Luis Eduardo Luna and Graham Hancock regarding the psycho-active properties of psilocybin and DMT (dimetyltryptamine) in relation to phenomena of consciousness. I would also like to mention an interesting observation regarding this by William Braden (the father of Gregg) who, talking about the 'drug problem', in his book 'The Private Sea: LSD and the Search for God' (1967) writes: *'The real danger of acid is not that it will damage the brain, or that it will cause young people to drop out of society. We already live with drugs such as alcohol which produce effects like that. No, the real danger of acid is that some of its users claim that LSD puts them in contact with the illusory nature of the material world. The real danger of acid is that some freak will journey to the centre of things, discover the movie projector that is producing this illusion, and turn it off!'*

matter.[...] I am even more convinced that the answer to all of these mysteries that shake our classic view of the world is to be understood by looking inside ourselves.[...] The paths of the heart lead to nearby universes, full of life and benevolent feelings towards humanity. »

I feel it is important not to underestimate the para-physical (and esoteric[7]) interpretation of a phenomenon, that is certainly and undeniably becoming more 'frequent', in the search for the key to its manifestation.

The universe is a product of our consciousness and a projection of our senses: we are at one with the Absolute which, for some reason, presents itself in the form of different frequencies of energy and consciousness. They relate to one another and create, in our case, the image that constitutes our plane of existence and which appears to be three-dimensional and oriented in uni-directional time.

According to some, we (and our lives) are *Maya*, illusion, as portrayed in the film 'Matrix'; according to others however, doubt cannot be cast upon our existence or at least our form of existence, which is significant in itself.
Reality could be positioned somewhere in between: we find ourselves in an illusion (and it is always good to remember that) which is nevertheless our reality (so we cannot possibly deny it).

All things considered it is better to not be hasty in drawing conclusions about the UFO phenomenon and the nature of 'alien' interference or even pretend to have definitively

---

[7] Actually Crowley was amongst the first to experiment with peyote (which he took from Mexico to London) for magic purposes at the beginning of the last century!

understood its nature or intentions (or 'agenda'). The origin of such interference is not yet clear and definitive, just as the nature of the reality that we define as 'physical' and 'material' is not yet clear, especially when related to the dynamics of our psyche. And as William Shakespeare so aptly says in *Hamlet,* "There are more things in heaven and earth Horatio, than are dreamt of in your philosophy."

We ourselves can be said to exist on a certain plane of existence, which is manifested and projected through dynamics that are not yet completely decoded. This 'existing' is nevertheless confined inside rather limited parameters and our current existence will in all probability result as being fictitious when compared in a broader sense.

Those wider parameters could relate to our nature which is likewise much more expansive than we realize and what is currently considered as supernatural or alien could, on another level, be the natural expression of reality and ourselves.

Our existence is played out in a sensorial circuit that we need to control and decrypt in order to give reality a chrism of truthfulness despite the fact that our senses are vibrating and testing that reality on the same frequencies. Although our senses give us the sensation of reality in all its physicality, it is only equivalent to its existential 'plane'.

We are living at a historical moment in which culture and values are being re-examined and the same esoteric dimensions are being mixed together to reformulate a concept of reality: in this sense we are perhaps on the threshold of great changes.

We will go into the themes inherent in parallel worlds and the 'separation of the planes' in Appendix II. It is increasingly obvious that the certainties of our global village which have been consolidated up to now, be they material or spiritual, are disintegrating and re-organizing according to potential schemes that could take off in many different directions[8].

To describe their form I scatter rhymes no more,
 reader, for other expense binds me
so, that in this I cannot be lavish.
But read Ezekiel, for he depicts them
as he saw them come from the cold quarter
with wind, with cloud, with fire;

Dante Alighieri - Purgatorio Canto XXIX, 97-102

Esoteric Physics and Modern Physics

In contemporary Physics *strings*[9] are infinitesimal particles of matter. Scientific research, with the use of increasingly

---

[8] The position of the renowned academic and populariser Igor Sibaldi is also significant as regards this point – he talks about the nature of the Angel and Spirit Guides as 'higher' aspects of our own nature and of our trans-human psyche, individually and collectively. This perspective obliges us to re-examine the concept and practice of mediums (contactism or channelling if you want to call it that) and consider such phenomena as an instrument of transpersonal introspection. I will also take this opportunity to quote the following observation from Sibaldi: "The goal to aim for is a new dimension of existence in which each person dreams to set foot and finally be themselves, no longer prisoners of rigid, dangerous everyday schemes, no longer at the mercy of absurd prejudices and arid ways of thinking that stop them from being happy".

[9] In physics, 'String Theory' is currently under development and aims to reconcile quantum mechanics with general relativity and seems to have all

powerful accelerators, has obtained an immense quantity of data on the constitution of matter. *String Theory* proposes that all particles emerge from different types of interaction between strings and are held in four constituent families of matter. However, in contracting, stable or infinitely expanding models of the universe, the quantity of matter necessary to justify its existence does not meet with experimental observation. The missing part, defined as 'dark matter' still awaits the right theoretical setting, which may or may not result as definable. Therefore it will not necessarily be rational research that justifies the nature of existence and or its reasons for being. We can also assume the burden of such research and claim the right to adopt a different approach to its problems; alternative methods can be just as dignified as classic ones if conducted with common sense and enthusiasm.

In its current state it would seem that less than 5% of the universe comprises normal particles, protons and neutrons leaving the rest of the universe made up of, as yet, unrevealed constituents. Looking at it in extreme synthesis, we can say the theory of 'dark matter' states, of all the matter-energy in play in the cosmos only 4-5% is visible: the galaxies, planets, we ourselves, and the light and heat of the stars. More or less 23% is formed from dark matter and the remaining 73% by dark energy. The parallel between an awareness of reality and an awareness of ourselves becomes clearly evident. It is said that we use only 5% of our brains, 5% of our DNA (scientists are asking themselves what the rest is for, or even if it is 'waste'!) and we are only conscious of ourselves 5% of the time and, that

---

the necessary characteristics for becoming a 'Theory of Everything'. It is founded on the principle in which matter, energy and under certain hypotheses, space and time are manifestations of physical entities below which, according to the number of dimensions they develop in, they are called 'Strings'.

51

is on a good day. It is natural that in such conditions, we only perceive 5% of reality: all the rest is 'dark'.

Paradoxically, however, it is We (that is our constantly active and operating consciousness) who create reality. All of it.
Always and entirely with the totality of ourselves, whether we are aware of it or not.

A precise correspondence exists between the awareness of what we are and the perception of the reality that surrounds us, given that the latter is nothing more than an extension of ourselves! English novelist Henry M. Tomlinson said that: "We see things not as they are but as we are ourselves". This is what we do on our plane of existence, at the level of our current consciousness, which is limited, vulnerable and programmable. Therefore the un-conscious with all its hopes and fears is nothing more than the unsuspected extension of ourselves in the *'Great Beyond'*, with all its angels, demons entities and monsters: it is nothing more than our own dark matter, with all its aliens and mysteries! And for those who are interested in global control and manipulation, the unconscious must always remain in a limited state; otherwise we would reawaken to the infinite consciousness of which we are all the expression and fulfilment!

This is why – in as much as we are human beings – we are so important, so unique: because it is within our power to create reality, any kind of reality. So important in fact that, those who are signalled out by the various esoteric cultures as our jailers (subtle, dimensional, alien etc...), actually have great need of us because the power to forge reality was only given to us humans, though at a higher level of awareness than our current one.

Therefore all 'they' have to do is encourage us to create the most suitable reality for them. It is made strong through of our lack of conscious awareness and they nourish themselves on it, prospering from the reality that we have created. We are totally brainwashed by their systems of persuasion, which slowly assign us the role of dominator on the one hand and dominated on the other.

The concepts of parallel worlds, echo-worlds and ultra light, contemporary and interpenetrating planes of existence have always been part of ancient cosmogonist traditions and likewise the complex conception of the human being and its soul.

Some recent considerations by modern astrophysicists, on the problem of the missing mass (in which the effects of gravitation are revealed), lead us to consider the possibility of interference from hypothetical, parallel or hyper-compressed worlds, which perhaps in turn constitute a multi-dimensional super-world: This is the *Real* as seen by physicists. Contrary to prevailing theories of physics our kind of metaphysics privileges a coherent and undulatory vision of reality that is not at all indeterministic.

In the infinitely small – just as at all scales – the mechanism of creation and universal evolution renews itself. It is well known that matter consists of more void than content and according to esoteric thought, in every atom, in every quark and even in the tiniest particle of matter that we might care to consider, it renews itself continuously, instant by instant, on all planes *from inside* the dynamics of the void, energy and creation.

Every object, whether it be living or inanimate, infinitesimal or gigantic, elementary or complex, has its own material parts, energy, subtle bodies, soul and spiritual essence at a level of self-awareness in proportion to its biological and existential complexity.

Inside the material world the clash between the void and time is renewed, the fundamental laws are modulated on various scales and, just as the macrocosm is sensitive to the 'Mind of God', in its smallness, every object is sensitive to the mind of the *inner god* in each one of us when opportunely conscious and operative.

The power of the mind lies in the power of creation and the transformation of the universal hologram at different levels, from illusion (*the power of Maya*, as the Hindus call it) to the intrinsic reality of all things. Transformations are achieved when we ourselves apply our reawakened consciousness to reality and know how to lead it back to the Absolute Being, to the One, to the Real.

The Mind, or better still the use of real Thought, creates and determines everything moment by moment. It creates and determines the One and each and every single part in simultaneous harmony. That Mind, that Power, permeates all things: it is everywhere, it operates everywhere. We, you and I, each one of us is a channel for this power which creates everything.

Rol, the famous Italian psychic, maintained that he was able to enter into contact with the 'intelligent spirit' of each and every thing and to have therefore discovered the true secret of the Universe, in virtue of his reawakened spirit, by overcoming the barrier of physical laws. This was basically the secret of his power over the material world.

Just as the *derivative laws* are consolidated around the primordial essence (the peak) and in order to climb, mass on successive levels of reality (time matrices, natural laws etc.), our identities (divine, mental, astral, biological etc.) collect around our inner spiritual essence, similar to the constellations of the zodiac – not by chance adopted by the ancients to reflect our characters – around a central Sun.

From the real to the transcendent, from God, who creates and transforms the infinite, to you who are creating and leafing through this book, the same mechanism is expressed. The same power.

The Functions and Archetypes of our Universe

Our universe is a balanced field of *functions* (laws) that originate in broader pre-universal mechanics. They are not yet the fundamental laws discovered by physics but something further upstream. The fundamental functions of our universe could be associated with the creative aspects of the Sephiroth – or, if you prefer, the Trigrams of the I Ching – and in microcosm with the system of the *chakra*.

Using other methods, perhaps more direct and radical, native populations and shamans describe, the same dynamics that we are summarizing here in their first-hand experience and 'visions' in altered states of consciousness[10], representing them

---

[10] It would be true to say that the most altered state of consciousness is really that of our daily lives which is absurd in comparison to the states of ecstasy and meditation that undoubtedly correspond to more authentic perceptions of the self and reality.

through an archaic symbolism which is mysterious and yet immediate and absorbing.

According to Western esoteric tradition there are thought to be *eight fundamental functions* which once translated into time matrices and physical laws relate to one another by means of *24 archetypes*.

There are various numerations and classifications: based on 2 or 4 (usually applied to the material and human world), based on 12 (on a cosmic scale, in the case of the eons of Gnostic tradition), based on 3 or 7 (usually applied to the divine dimensions in relation to human 'types') or based upon the omnipresent sequence of Fibonacci (applied to Sacred Geometry and the so-called Golden Section) and all their possible combinations. It is useful to take a look at those aspects which more or less act as a background to all the others.

One of the most significant hermetic compendiums, the *Kybalion*[11], lists the following seven fundamental principles:

1.   *Principle of mentalism*, or 'all is mind'.
2.   *Principle of correspondence*: there is always a correspondence between the phenomena of various planes of

---

[11] We are talking about an essay of Hermetic philosophy published in the United States in 1908, the work of 'Three Initiates', formally indicated as written by anonymous authors even though it is almost certain that they were William W. Atkinson (who had already published work under the pseudo name of Yogi Ramacharaka, (a name borrowed perhaps from his former oriental master), Paul F. Case (member of the Golden Dawn and founder of a schismatic movement) and Mabel Collins, the noted Theosophist and pupil of Helena P. Blavatsky, author of the fundamental occult treatise *Light on the Path*.

existence (physical, mental and spiritual), in deference to the principle 'as above so below'.

3. *Principle of vibration*: nothing is still, everything is in movement and vibration.

The differences between the material, the mind, energy and the spirit can be reduced to vibrational disparity: the higher the evolutionary level the higher the vibrational frequency. The All (the Absolute, the Supreme Mind) has an infinitely high vibrational level. The art of mental transformation rests precisely in the art of modifying the vibrational state: a result that is achieved through the exertion of the will.

4. *Principle of polarity*: everything is dual, everything has two poles, and everything has its opposite. Every thing 'is' and 'is not' at the same time, every truth is nothing more than a half truth and half falsehood at the same time. Opposites share the same nature but in different degrees, extremes touch one another and all possible paradoxes can be reconciled.

5. *Principle of rhythm*: in all things there is movement similar to that of a pendulum. This principle explains how there is a rhythm in every pair of opposites or poles and is therefore closely linked to the Principle of polarity.

6. *Principle of cause and effect*: there is a cause for every effect and an effect for every cause. Chaos does not exist: 'chaos' is just the name given to non-identifiable or perceivable causes.

7. *Principle of gender*: everything has a gender, masculine or feminine. This concept has nothing to do with sexual gender. Mental gender is in fact free and independent of the sexual or physical gender of a person. The masculine gender is active, projected externally, and its key word is 'Will'. The feminine gender is receptive, creates new thought and ideas and its key word is 'Imagination'. There has to be a balance between the two genders: In fact, the masculine if not balanced by the feminine, acts indiscriminately and inclines towards chaos, just as the feminine if not balanced by the masculine tends to

stagnate. Masculine and feminine together create sound action that leads to success.

To these seven fundamental principles, which are obviously developed from the classical hermetic principles attributed to Hermes Trismegistus, I would add a more implicit, or if you prefer *occult* eighth: *Synchronicity*. The 24 archetypes are without doubt related to, but not only, the 24 Major Arcana of the Tarot (therefore not 22), a profound knowledge of which can be found by beginning with the classical deck of Eliphas Levi and then later studying the 22+2 Arcana of Crowley.

It is necessary to awaken the Consciousness in ourselves – or better still to *wake up* to that Consciousness. In order to do that we have to recover the lost archetypes, rehabilitate our Energy and our inner faculties and reconnect our spiritual parts to our soul. We have to recover the *hardware* (archetypes) and the *software* (energy, senses and faculties) emancipating ourselves from every limit and received conditioning through a process of transformation which is both mental and corporeal.

We can thus explore and evolve through the manifestations of reality, and all that is set out here will be *seen* as natural and evident. Our objective however, is not to become programmers of the illusion but to understand reality through all its possible illusions.

The eight functions or *universal laws*, set out in a conventional and logical sequence should be related to the principles listed below with their corresponding hermetic attribute:

1. *Frequency* – the principle of vibration
2. *Interaction* – the principle of cause and effect
3. *Sacred Geometry* – the principle of correspondence

4. *Immanent consciousness* – the principle of mentalism
5. *Correspondence* – the principle of rhythm
6. *Synchronicity* – the hidden principle
7. *Chaos* – the principle of polarity
8. *Arrow of Complexity* – the principle of gender

Every universe has its own 'local' laws, which in the case of our universe we calculate as being eight. Outside our field of interest it makes no sense to number something other than for allegorical representation. There is no point in numbering the primeval laws or the *laws of another universe* or the primeval emanations of Consciousness. At those levels the concept of numbers loses all significance.

From the eight basic functions, all the successive energetic, dimensional and space-time dynamics are triggered and therefore the laws that on our specific plane of existence are described, for lack of a more elegant and all encompassing formula, as electromagnetic, gravitational and strong or weak nuclear forces.

These metaphysics are a kind of pre-quantum physics rather than a transcendental physics.

Universal Functions	Sephiroth	Chakra	Emotions		Faculties	Mantra	Attitude	Buddhism	Ashtanga Yog
			Positive	Negative					
Frequency	Malkuth	coccyx	happiness	unhappiness	dimensions/aura	A	action	right action	Yama
Interaction	Yesod	genitals	security	insecurity	memory	E1	continuity-coherence	right mindfulness	Nyama
Sacred Geometry	Hod/Netzach	plexus	joy	suffering	mind	E2	depth	right concentration	Asana
Immanent Consciousness	Tipheret	heart	love	hate	intent	O1	welcome-availability	right intention	Pranayama
Correspondence	Geburah/Chesed	throat	gaiety	sadness	para-telepathy	O2	exploration-movement	right effort	Pratyahara
Synchronicity	Daath	"mobile"	completeness	defeat	emotions	IAOUE-EUOAI	art-creativity	right speech	Dharana
Chaos	Binah/Chockmah	3rd eye	serenity	restlessness	dream	U	renovation-adaptability	right livelihood	Dyana
Complexity	Kether	crown	beatitude	anguish	consciousness	I	sharing-generation	right view	Samadhi

Now consider the following table, which will be looking at again in the course of our assessment. You will see the fundamental functions of our universe (derivative laws) listed and their correlation to certain elements of different esoteric disciplines.

For a more in-depth look at the nature and functions of each derivative law please consult Appendix I.

The Subtle Anatomy of the Human Being

Man is capable of being and using anything which he perceives, for everything that he perceives is in a certain sense a part of his being. He may thus subjugate the whole Universe of which he is conscious to his own individual Will.
Magick is the Science of understanding oneself and one's conditions. It is the Art of applying that understanding in action.

Aleister Crowley - Magick in Theory and Practice

Subtle Bodies and Energy Flows

Just as our planetary system is reached by cosmic currents through the Synchronic and Telluric Lines (*leylines*) and is sensitive to *morphogenetic* fields, our body is also traversed by as many currents and lines of energy.

To be precise we are considering a series of traditions and perceptions, of a sensitivity which does not form part of Western materialism, which have been reported in esoteric accounts and spiritualistic visions of human reality. It would be incongruous to reduce such concepts to the terrain of today's accepted science: it is not possible and perhaps it is not pertinent. Such concepts cannot be approached with the logic and instruments of our so called 'orthodox' modern science. We can however, perceive them at a personal and subjective level or find them described in accounts and traditions which are considered primitive and superstitious and are perhaps undervalued.

We are in fact talking about the cultural heritage of humanity which deserves our respect and should not be hastily cast aside on the basis of current scientific dictates.

In Eastern tradition, in particular that of India, the *chakra represent* the principal meeting points of all our energy flows, or more exactly of the massive network of information and energy that courses through us. They are the points of convergence and connection between all our different natures: psycho-physical, soul (emotive, mental, emotional), spiritual and divine. Our endocrine system is associated to them, our physical apparatus and organs and all aspects of our way of being and living.

Every chakra is the engine, filter and valve, of the system of subtle energy flows found inside and outside of the body.

Bearing this in mind we can make a distinction between:

- Meridians and linear chains
- Microlines
- Lines of force
- Temporal flows
- Subtle geometries

Just as our reality – and the Form that is part of it – can be, in the final analysis, reduced to three fundamental states of being (physical-subtle-spiritual), in the same way the human being can be considered as the point of convergence of three fundamental natures:

1. The *physical body*
2. The *soul*, seen as a structure made up of different experiences and individual personalities and from another point of view, perceivable as a complex of

62

thoughts/sensations/experiences described in the form of bodies and subtle geometries
3. The *spirit*, the profound aspect present in all things which leads back to the All. In the case of a bio-psycho-spiritual complex (*bridge-Form*) such as ours, the spirit is the gateway and transmitter of the divine spark, understood as a superior active identity capable of self-awareness and transcendence.

Metaphorically speaking we can say that the body is like a tape recorder, the spirit is the magnetic tape, the soul is the recording and consciousness is the act of listening to the recording.

Subtle Energies and Electromagnetic Prisons

As we have seen, the universe of Form manifests according to precise patterns: from ideas to archetypes, from archetypes to numbers and from numbers to dimensions and material phenomena.

Material Form and events represent the multi-dimensional manifestation of a *holographic* universe whose fundamental geometries are recognizable in the infinitely small just as they are in the infinitely large.
Through these recurring geometries every expression of the universe is by correspondence, united to all others, regardless of dimension, temporal and spatial distance.

The *aura* is not only that bio-radiant body that can be verified through the use of the Kirlian Camera, but something much more complex and subtle, that can be seen by employing a higher level of sensitivity.

Our physical body, in turn constituted from its more external parts (subtle and soft) to its bone structure, is the central massing of a system of subtle bodies in movement. As if it were interpenetrating crystals mounted on a pivot and made to rotate. In the same way our subtle geometries rotate around the body following directional flows, speeds and different rhythms, generating a particular 'optical' effect that is typical of a spinning top: a halo in the shape of an egg.
This is the aura that clairvoyants perceive by translating the results of their perception into colours (into the sense of vision) which, in fact leads to other senses which do not translate into ocular vision as such.

All subtle structures are profoundly linked to our mind and to the functions of our body. They have been classified differently according to the perspectives and needs of individual schools of thought. The model most frequently referred to is that of Theosophy, of which an infinite number of re-elaborations have been made.

Theosophy (think of the specific treatises of Arthur E. Powel) – elaborating on the Hindu tradition but also that of neoplatonic-Hermeticism – describes a series of 'bodies' or 'vehicles' of consciousness that interpenetrate and envelop the physical body. In each one dwells the divine principle, at different levels of self-awareness and which nevertheless expands beyond them.

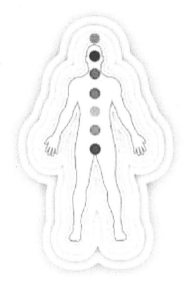

The Etheric body (bio-magnetic)

The first of the subtle bodies that lies outside the physical body is its 'etheric field'. It is the home of the vital force that sustains the life of the physical body and acts as a matrix for its metabolic functions. It is on this that different kinds of bio-energetic therapies intervene. It is the halo that can be seen with the Kirlian Camera.

The Astral Body

The 'astral body' is a sort of mental or psychic (sometimes defined as the *inferior mental body*), it is this that we refer to when we talk about 'Out of Body Experiences' (OBE) or 'astral travel'. The personalities of the soul's structure are for the most part connected to this body. The word astral is used in a traditional sense to codify our behaviour and the nature of our personalities through astrology. When the aspects of a lower and more materialistic nature of the human personality are referred to, the astral body is defined as the 'body of desire', home to instincts and drives often judged as 'lower', not because they are typical of animals but because they often lead to emotivity and egoistic needs.

The Mental Body

This is the body of thoughts and the intellect. After death, it is the survivor of the ego, the central individuality that has evolved best during physical life: it is the personality in formation that identifies the individual in his/her most evolved and integrated aspect, the basis of that everlasting identity that we will later define as 'intelligent spirit'.

The Mental or Causal Superior Body

This is the body of higher spiritual inspiration which corresponds to the crown *chakra*. It is the 'spirit': the part in each one of us that leads back to the All, or to the Absolute Being in its totality. It is also our centre of consciousness: The divine identity that we are but which is reawakened through the human experience in the material world of Form.

Each of these subtle bodies corresponds to a particular plane or world of existence. For the 'astral body' there is the 'astral plane', just as for the 'mental body' there is the 'mental plane' and so on.

Shown below an interesting image found on various web sites which illustrates the idea that what we consider to be 'inside' and 'outside' of us is really a mirror image.

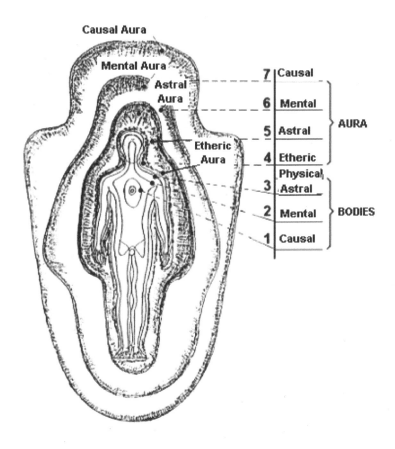

The subtle bodies are generated and nourished by our system of beliefs and our convictions about ourselves and life. They are therefore in line with our mental dynamics which, from a certain point of view, generally correspond to the characteristics of the electromagnetic field of our materialness. They are however, more specifically linked to planetary 'electromagnetism', which is currently being subjected to manipulation through advanced instruments of global control.

We are sensitive to and conditioned by streams of thought, by fluctuations in the density of time-space and magnetism. If something should disturb the Earth's magnetic equilibrium in 2012 it will without doubt have repercussions on our perceptive-existential system and, even though for some it might be an apocalypse, for others it will be an opportunity to benefit from a moment of vulnerability in the 'matrix' and liberate themselves from the deception of the mind and this pseudo-reality.

We have been so conditioned by a fear of the void and death that we cling on to the illusions that have been instilled into us, even to perceptions about what it means to exist: if we think, we exist, if we have ideas and projects and a recognized role. Otherwise we do not. This is a terrible form of blackmail.

This is because we only identify our state of existence with a sensorial perception of the physical world, without knowing – or even intuiting – that by doing so we distance ourselves even more from true being and real happiness.

Humanity is at a crossroads: we either find the core of our identity and therefore a profound sense of life and reality or we degenerate into the irreversible madness of self-destruction and inevitable narcosis: intimately controlled by the structure of an ordered and conformist society, robotic and hypnotized by the latest and increasingly banal syncretic forms of a new hypocritical religion of well-being and universal goodness. If such a destiny fulfils itself, the dissolution of Mankind and its society will quickly follow. The Universe, by means of its laws, will then re-establish the equilibriums that have been contaminated by Mankind which are necessary for life and evolution.

That new equilibrium is on the horizon and if we do not want to be swept away by history, we need to shake off the apathy and torpor that originates from being dependent on a hyper-dynamic and hyper-productive state of reality that is increasingly disconnected and inconsistent.

The Light Body

Today one hears talk of faculties and 'bodies' that are reawakened, enlightened and brought into consciousness, or built through particular meditation techniques in order to access the spiritual possibilities that the New Era will open up to the human population of Earth. It is a term that is often used but 'Light Body' is certainly not a new term to esoteric tradition.

Traditionally – in Western magic practices – the Light Body corresponds to the conscious body that is used by the 'magician' to travel between the dimensions of time and space and, beyond such dimensions into the 'astral' worlds to reach the higher planes of Self-Awareness and Absolute Being. It is a kind of 'astral body' but much more evolved and sublime as a concept.

Today we talk of the Light Body instead of referring to our being in a state of complete awareness, in all its physical, subtle and spiritual constituents. In fact, according to the most commonly accepted concept of *ascension*, it is our physical transubstantiated body at a superior level of existence and awareness, that will effectively permit access to a more authentic and more 'luminous' level of reality that is more real and less obscured by the psycho-physical illusions in which we are now ensnared.

Meridians, Microlines and Temporal Flows

The meridians (the 72,000 *Nadi*) have been carefully investigated by Eastern traditions and even today are of interest to a major part of traditional medicine such as acupuncture, *Shiatzu* and chromo-puncture. They are energetic and bio-magnetic flows and by working on them it is possible to re-establish particular equilibriums that will stimulate certain faculties and help individuals achieve a state of harmony and health. Disease is basically interpreted as a problem in the body's internal communications system. From this view point, using the correct instruments or massage, it is possible to 'unblock' certain channels of energy flows and encourage the re-establishment of natural correspondences between the subtle and the physical and thereby recuperate – and conserve –an optimum state of health.

The Nadi are subtle inner pathways which are thought to be the conductors of the vital energy, Prana. The three most important Nadi are: *Ida*, *Pingala* and *Sushumna*.

They are set out like a caduceus in as much as *Sushumna* is the centre channel while *Ida* and *Pingala* flow respectively to the right and left, crossing it at determined heights.

Ida is connected with the *feminine polarity* while Pingala is connected to that of the *masculine*.

Eastern traditions state that when meditators withdraw their attention from their surroundings and retreat inside the self, striving through psychic and physical practices to recover the mystery which lies within, reawaken the *Kundalini*, the cosmic potency sleeping inside those who have forgotten their true essence.

This reawakening – which in certain circumstances can also happen spontaneously or be caused by particular circumstances (for example the phenomena of mysticism) and often eludes the comprehension or control of its protagonists – is usually accompanied by a blast of energetic heat and considered rather dangerous.

There are many schools which prefer a more progressive and harmonious road to reawakening rather than a direct and vehement one, this permits the Kundalini to reawaken in a natural way so that the energy derived from it can be consciously managed.

At various heights on the vertebral column we find the *chakra*, also defined as *Padma* (lotus), which supervise the body's activities. They function in relation to the body's psychic sphere and in its universal processes and also in relation to the identity which exists between the microcosm/Mankind and the macrocosm/Universe.

Trying to achieve expanded consciousness by working directly on the reawakening of the *Kundalini* is very dangerous because this latent cosmic force if it is well channelled invigorates and transforms, but if an individual is not ready to deal with its impact, can burn, overwhelm and even result in madness and death

If however it is correctly controlled, *Kundalini* transforms the human body into a 'divine body'. The tangible manifestations of such a process, appear to be the so called *Siddhi*, the 'perfections', or those supernatural powers realized by the human being that have full control over baser instincts.

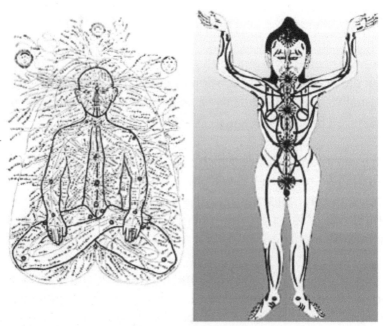

The nadi as illustrated in traditional Indian and Chinese texts

The microlines, whose position in the body is very different to that of the meridians, constitute a more subtle an essential network of flows of vital and spiritual energies and 'interface', as it were, our superior consciousness with the reality of events or with our current dimension.

The microlines allow our subtle bodies to move according to their different needs. They form in the fourth month of pregnancy and can form and develop by means of their own inner faculties.

The microlines flow on the body and in the body, both on the surface and at different depths and intensify in the hands, the ears and by correspondence in the eyes. Vital energies flow in the microlines first and are later processed by the chakra.

Sometimes the microlines assume positions which are partly external in respect to physical posture, enough even to project themselves outside of the aura. They tend to arrange themselves harmonically in respect to the movement of the body and usually coordinate themselves by anticipating the physical movements of the body itself.

Particular dances exist (think of all the sacred dances of the world from the tribal to the religious, from types of bio-dance to yoga, from the dances of the Sufi to the *Tensegrity* that Castaneda talks about) and specific techniques of 'harmonization' through which we can direct the circuits of the microlines to maintain, receive or exchange energy. We are talking about archetypical movements and positions of great importance that allow the centres of vital energy to be stimulated.

The microlines do not position themselves on immovable tracks but modify their positions following a kind of (bio) rhythm that lasts around seventy days.
It is also important to note that individual choices, above all those of a spiritual nature, can modify the subtle design of the person (and vice versa).

The microlines are nourished by vital energy, so it is important to maintain a harmonious contact with life: eat naturally and healthily, live in contact with nature or regenerate every now and again in a natural environment, for example by taking a long walk in the woods. A healthy and natural life has much more value than meditation techniques (and medicine). Precise massage techniques also exist which can be practiced by pregnant women to promote the harmonious development of the subtle bodies of the unborn child.

The microlines find a correspondence in the *Synchronic Lines* of the planet and are sensitive to the lines to which they are geographically closest. Just as with the Synchronic Lines, the microlines are divided into major and minor lines and microlines of different intensity can also be distinguished in the human body.

The chakra constitute the *nodes* of the major microlines and correspond to the planetary synchronic nodes that can be imagined as the chakra of the Earth. If we want to draw parallels we could think of a *standing stone* which functions as a kind of acupuncture on the body of the planet.

The microlines are closely related to the major Synchronic Lines: in theory by acting on the Synchronic Lines we can act by correspondence on somewhere else in the world: we create a correspondence in the people who live in that place by means of their microlines. We are talking about a rather complex level of alchemy which is currently being investigated by certain centres of power, ready to exploit its potential in order to control and manipulate the masses. But the opposite is also true: by working properly on oneself it is possible to produce changes on the planet at a synchronic level.

74

In order to interact with the subtle and vital reality that surrounds us, we project our *lines of force* by means of thirty-three valves positioned in the aura which correspond with precise points on the subtle geometries that surround the physical body. These lines are perceived by magicians and shamans during their altered states of consciousness and are 'seen' as blue currents of energy that project in and from the body (as testified by various magicians during my stay in Cameroon).

We can also say that we emit these lines of force from the 'nodes' of our microlines which then connect with the geometry of events. They create a sort of energetic cobweb, attracting or repelling energies, forces and thoughts that are more or less in tune with our nature and our will.

In effect, by moving our *'point of union'* (the *assemblage point* as Castaneda called it) we can create or give shape to the reality which surrounds us through our system of microlines and lines of force.

Another system of currents known as *temporal flows*, is acknowledged by certain Eastern schools, although perhaps not in these terms. Through this particular system we are connected to the structure of time. Time is not a dimension linked to the world of material Form but develops its own 'field' and is governed by autonomous laws. It is a dimension with its own reason for being which regardless of the world of Form constitutes the indispensible ramifications of 'support' on which the material dimensions (space and Form) manifest.
Time is a complex, intelligent and *independent eco-system*, we could even say 'living', with which the diverse possible manifestations of existence are in strict symbiosis. We ourselves are, more than anything else, all *temporal beings* and

75

relate to time through a special connection: the *temporal flows* to be precise. The most important thing to remember is that by means of the temporal flows a 'substance' reaches us that is fundamental to our evolution: that substance is called *thought*.

As is well explained in the *Treatise on Living Thought* by Massimo Scaligero, thought is not something that we produce through the dynamics of the mind but a substance in which we are immersed and that we are limited to processing only at our own level of awareness. There exists a strict correlation between the density of the temporal fabric and the quantity of accessible thought, furthermore our reality it is qualitively proportional to the quality of the thought substance that we 'inhale'. However, this thought is also the target of programmes that condition our minds.

A correct method of breathing is a useful procedure for the purification and detoxification of such conditioning. It is also a way to activate *Prana* channels and access a level of interaction with thought and the universal mind which is way above our current possibilities. By applying special massage or breathing techniques, we can balance and regulate the flow of thoughts that pass through us along the temporal body flows, notably improving the quality of our elaboration. This process reflects upon how we interpret ourselves and reality itself.
Let's not forget that in ancient civilizations, in particular that of Egypt, the different functions of thought were positioned in more than one part of the body, in particular, besides the brain, in the intestine and the heart. Many meditation techniques have been individuated to develop the capacity to process thought, from the use of lateral thinking to emotive intelligence, but the most important role is that played by Art.
Art is the best instrument for the glorification of our talents and our creativity but most of all our ability to reawaken the

intelligence of the body which is much more complete than that of the 'rational' mind.

The Chakra

The principle connection points between one state and another of our being are constituted by the *chakra* whose access can be found along the spine to the top of the head and beyond (the *Onios Channel*). Knowledge of the Chakra belongs to the Hindu, Jainist and Buddhist traditions spread throughout the West by Theosophy. However certain Western treatises exist in which one can presume there was also a knowledge of these 'centres of force' on the part of alchemists and mystical Christians such as Jacob Bhome (1575-1624) and some of his pupils, in particular Johann Georg Gichtel (1638-1710), author of *Practical Theosophy* (1727)[12].

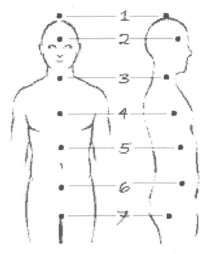

Every chakra is a multidimensional energetic node, a vortex of vital energy and a refinery of substances and faculties which correspond to specific physical organs, certain 'powers' and aspects of our way of being.

---

[12] The doctrine of the chakra was fully presented for the first time in the West by Sir John Woodroffe, when in 1917, under the pseudonym Arthur Avalon, he published 'The Serpent Power', or the translation of the Indian texts Sat-Cakra-Nirupana and Padaka-Pancaka.

Body	Chakra	Elements	Colour	Hz	Note	Tattwa
Physical	Muladhara	Earth	Red	256	C	Pritihivi
Etheric (bio-magnetic)	Svadhistana	Water	Orange	288	D	Apas
Etheric	Manipura	Fire	Yellow	323	E	Tejas
Astral	Anahata	Air	Green	342	F	Vayu
Body of Light (potential)	Vishuddha	Aether	Blue	384	G	Akasha
Mental	Ajna	Thought	Indigo	432	A	Maha
Causal	Sahasrara	Spirit	Violet Gold	484	B	

This is a simple reference table for the seven traditional chakra with some particular correspondences that I feel are useful for practical purposes[13].

Many Schools propose models based on a greater number of chakra (let's not forget that there are hundreds of chakra in the body: many researchers also consider that there are many more 'major' chakra than those represented by the Tradition)[14].

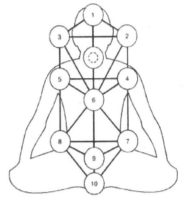

At the end of our current examination we will consider *eight* basic chakra. The eighth chakra – mentioned in various practical studies – is the resultant product of the other seven which are in harmony with one another. It is also defined as 'mobile' because it moves around according to determined stimuli and functions. Its principle function is that of 'turning on' the other seven, according to specific working methods. Other traditions have identified these fundamental

---

[13] Note the use of the musical scale intonated on A=432 Hz, which corresponds to the entire musical scale intonated on the basis of frequencies in tune with universal and cosmic harmonies, as were employed before the reforms of the 1950's enforced tuning to 440 Hz, which in fact distorts the use and reception of sound provoking disharmonious effects on the environment and the body.

[14] Today it is perhaps useful to consider 12 chakra, 12 threads of DNA and 12 'rays'. However as it is still in the personal experimentation stage, I feel it is premature to speak of it here. On the question of DNA readers can consult my previous book *Nothing but Oneself*. Meanwhile, for further information on 'rays' - which represent another system of reading reality and physical and spiritual energies – I suggest specific Theosophical and post-Theosophical texts (in particular the works of H.P. Blavatsky, Alice Bailey and Douglas Baker).

points of force by overlaying the human design with the Sephirotic Tree in different ways.

To conclude, the chakra process and transform our vital energy on the basis of necessary functions. They connect the different physical, psychic, subtle and divine states that constitute our being, nourishing the exercise of our senses and higher faculties. By the latter we mean those inner faculties that originate in the divine spark, which allow a higher awareness to be projected on reality, emancipated from the constraints and the 'outward appearances' of the physical senses.

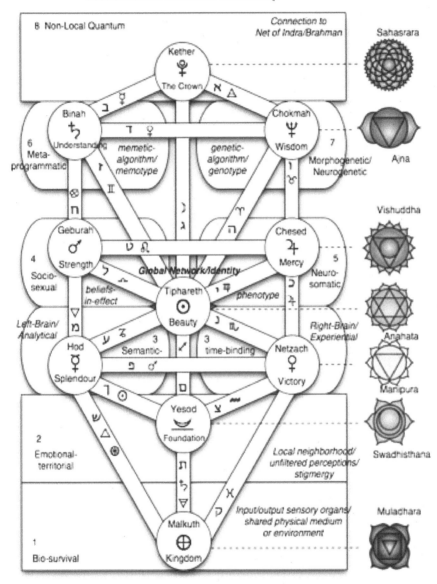

Qabala/Chakra/8-Dimension Model Mixup

Image courtesy of:
http://technoccult.net/archives/2004/12/20/qabalachakra8-dimensions-of-consciousness-mapped/

The Inner Faculties

The five accepted normal senses are not much use for perceiving how to select the frequencies of reality and determine the physical boundaries of our plane *of existence*. This means that our ability to describe natural phenomena and to understand reality is in fact proportional to the senses and logic we are able to employ.

On average at this level of existence, our current power of perception/determination is considerably reduced in respect to the real possibilities of our senses.

These powers of perception include those ESP faculties that para-psychological studies talked about at great length in the 1970's – 80's for example: telepathy, clairvoyance or clairaudience, pre- (or retro) cognition, the sensitivity and the properties of the aura and the astral body, the thaumaturgic and psycho-kinetic faculties of mediums that are part of a lost potency but ideally form part of our natural capacities.
There is nothing 'paranormal' about it at all. It is we who now operate below *normal* capacity, so much so that when we occasionally exercise those faculties or hear them talked about they seem to be something miraculous, if not to be feared and repressed.

Of a different nature though are the faculties that are specifically 'spiritual', those that have something to do with an extra-dimensional sensitivity in respect to our plane of psychic and physical existence, even when they are simply considered at their different and more extended vibrational and dimensional levels. Such capacities are linked to mystic phenomena and investigated specifically by magic and shamanism.

The optimum expression of our spiritual faculties, now merely a potential, is strictly related to the esoteric concept of thought, that substantial external entity that is not produced by the activity of our brain.

The human being participates in a multi-dimensional eco-system of energy-thought: it receives thought which has been processed by 'lower' species and then processes that thought-food for higher species, inside a real 'food chain'. In our present condition we not only do not produce thought, we are unable to process reality in real-time.

When we consider that we are perceiving and thinking, we are in fact just *remembering* the perceptions and the processing of 'something' that the mind has already had time to adapt to its limits, or its system of beliefs and prejudices. This places us in the narrow-minded confines of a very convincing illusion.

Taking another look at the fundamental question that Gurdjieff insisted upon, if we live in an illusion of the mind, how can we 'be' and therefore 'act'?

The perception of the present, the border between the memory of the past and the forecast of the future according to preconceived and habitual patterns, is illusory. We live in the distorted memory of ourselves and in a reality that is just as retouched, conventional and restricted. Our system of thought is spoilt even more and distorted further by collective programmes of manipulation both cultural and scientific. Furthermore, as regards the latter, we need to ask ourselves, if apart from the intrinsic damage (medicinal, additive, chemical, vaccines, ELF waves etc...) there isn't perhaps some conscious planning behind it all which is the fruit of a hidden agenda.

We have to abandon our current system of thinking and completely rebuild our psychic *habitat*: perhaps phenomena connected to 2012 (and more widely related to the rise of a 'New Era') will stimulate our energetic centres, our endocrine system (pineal gland) and *upgrade the Matrix*, perhaps rendering the present system vulnerable. We could then avail ourselves of a reset in the flow of thought and take the opportunity to renew the layout of reality. An opportunity that will not be automatic but will need to be grasped at an individual level, by being suitably predisposed, emancipating from old patterns and above all mistrusting occasional 'redeemers'.

Re-adapting to the completeness of our senses we will perceive our world and ourselves more consciously, accessing a reality of a much higher level that we ourselves have determined.

However, even at higher levels we will only be managing the 'power of maya', or power over the illusion and not power over the spiritual reality that subtends every manifestation relative to the Absolute Being. To access that higher level of awareness, the so called 'nagual' perspective of existence, we have to reawaken our divine identity and its *faculties*.

Such 'superior' faculties are really the prerogative of those beings that host the active spiritual principle: the divine spark. These 'senses' are in fact divine attributes which are able to supply us with a holistic vision of the natural and spiritual eco-system in which we are immersed.

In the course of the book I will be briefly describing certain basic faculties that according to esoteric traditions were lost by the earthly human being in the course of a rather intricate epic. The story is told in the chronicles of 'alternative' history

84

through the figures of ancient myth: a history that is rich in references and which projects the human being way beyond this dimension.

A real comprehension of spiritual faculties presupposes their reawakening, so for now, we will have to settle for expressing ourselves in metaphor and using limited examples which of necessity lead us back to our current sensorial experience.

If the physical senses filter and determine the hologram-reality that surrounds us, the *inner* senses extract and project a transcendent meaning which leads human experience back to the divine and absolute source from which everything comes. As Don Juan, the Yaqui sorcerer and protagonist of the tales of Castaneda would say "The first, see things on this side of the bridge; the others see things on the other side: the first, have a *tonal* perspective while the others, a *nagual* perspective".

Nagual contrasts with *tonal*, which is seen as everything that can be explained and understood through the rational. The Nagual is a reality which transcends the purely intellectual and of which one can only be a witness: it is all that is found outside the dominion of the word and the concept. It is that inexplicable spirit of which one can only have direct experience.

For example, from the shamanistic point of view, dream is the capacity to perceive states of being which are beyond the physical. It is the eye of the transpersonal planes, as described by Ken Wilber in his *No Boundary*. It is the 'seeing' of the shaman.

For example *Dream* – not to be confused with the functions of dreaming as commonly intended[15] – is the sense that allows us to consciously move on the astral, subtle and spiritual plains. There we enter into contact with a more authentic essence of ourselves and all things, perceiving that their origins and nature are the same and sensing their evolutionary direction.

Dream allows us to explore the intermediate dimension between the material world of Form and the Real, from the dimensions of thought-forms to those of the emotions, from the astral planes to the dimensions of disincarnate souls, from subtle worlds to divine provinces.

But these are also nothing more than conventions for allocating the various possible 'significances' of reality value on a scale: from those closest to the material word to those which are more mysterious, ideal and spiritual.

All of this can be represented as transcendent and contemporaneously immanent and beyond, but it is also *inside*. The rehabilitation of the *sense of dream* can be encouraged by the use of astral travel, hypnosis and lucid dreaming techniques in a state of profound relaxation (today the subject of study through *Reconnection* and *Theta Healing* techniques), aimed at reducing the exercise of the external senses and encouraging the emergence of subtle perceptions[16].

---

[15] Besides constituting a mental dynamic studied at length by psychoanalysis, from the esoteric point of view it is a gateway to the lower and higher levels of our being. It is very important to learn to dream and practice remembering and guiding dreams with the use of oneiric and interpretive techniques, beginning from a personal perspective and symbolic ability. However, the spiritual faculty of the 'sense of dream' is a different level again; it can be considered as one of the soul's senses.

[16] States of dreaming or relaxation are, however, no longer indispensable for exercising the spiritual faculties once we have complete command over ourselves. In fact, at that point we can participate consciously and

Let's summarize some of the basic concepts of the phenomenon of *astral travel*.

The term 'astral' – borrowed from Theosophical traditions – is reductive in respect of the concept of out of body experiences or better still, *ultra-body* because we are not talking about 'relocation' as such but rather the extension the self and personal sensitivity.

Here are some useful parameters to focus on:

- It is not a power in itself, or a faculty, but a way to observe, interpret and describe a determined dynamic, that has something to do with our true nature in as much as it is infinite consciousness.
- It normally triggers during nocturnal sleep in a spontaneous and unconscious way.
- The experience is often translated into dreams through common or subjective symbolism, which are sometimes remembered and sometimes not.
- It can happen in altered states of consciousness caused by trauma, coma, drugs, the taking of psycho-active substances, meditation, fainting, anaesthesia, hypnosis and near-death experiences.
- Such dynamics are used to energetically regenerate the mind and our subtle bodies and re-order and metabolize experiences and information.
- Consciously directing the experience of astral travel constitutes an instrument for expanding the senses and the consciousness and for positioning oneself in a broader spiritual scenario.

---

contemporaneously in different states of being, simultaneously exercising all our senses. In other words we participate in a more expansive reality in virtue of our increased breadth of Consciousness.

- When the dynamic happens spontaneously and we are unaware of it, its energetic management and defences necessary are automatically triggered by our mind. However, when we train ourselves to consciously generate it, we have to re-learn how to direct it; in this case the techniques of relaxation or sleep/dreaming serve to lower the 'volume' of the physical senses in such a way as to activate an 'alternative' sensitivity that we can focus our attention and awareness on.

- The fear we experience is that typical of the unknown: besides, it is good to remember that when we find ourselves in 'alternative' dimensions, they are not aseptic, therefore if an individual has not worked on their energies, emotions and perceptions they may encounter *something* unclassifiable, that will then be removed by the conscious mind or clad in projections. What remains, even after the removal has occurred is the sensation of fear, regardless of the nature of the experience.

- Once the method has been mastered, there are various levels of practice: from the perceptive expansion of our own current dimension to the use of astral travel to explore other dimensions and finally, the expansion of consciousness as a natural extension of the self in the wakened state.

This journey is a moment of attenuation of our incarnation: a moment of re-connecting with our higher Self and therefore with all the parts of our soul, throughout the dimensions and time. Now is the moment to overturn concepts and move our 'point of union' or our centre of gravity towards our real identity and re-formulate the concept of 'astral travel' just as we need to reconsider numerous other subjects in the light of new paradigms.

We are already a Consciousness that divides itself up among many planes in order to explore this material dimension and evolve. When we assert ourselves to travel on the astral planes we are doing nothing more than ...returning home a little.

An interesting question we might ask is: which part of us 'separates'?
Which part 'exits' to explore? And as a result, what corresponding dimension is reached? Therefore, which part of ourselves do we have to train to reach precise dimensions, to have this true experience of spiritual growth?

This thought is also valid for mediumistic experiences: it is obvious that we 'vibrate' on the frequency of our level of consciousness and we are therefore in tune with the phenomena, events and dimensions that correspond to it. This is the result of the law of attraction - similar attracts similar, or the concordance of complexity (temporal concordance), today referred to as the 'law of attraction', a phenomenon much more complex and intriguing than simply attracting positive or negative events to yourself.

We tend to relate to organizations and worlds – to be precise to the teachings – that 'belong' to us. But it is not necessary to pursue para-Gnostic explorations, learn mediumistic techniques or various methods for inducing out of body experiences, what we really have to do is reawaken the different levels of our true identity.

If we get used to considering everything that we are the authors or spectators of from an exquisitely spiritual point of view, we will discover in ourselves and what surrounds us, our true divine nature; and on this path we can and must identify with all the infinite possibilities of creation.

Gustavo Adolfo Rol

In Thelemic tradition, which in this case draws on the explorations of John Dee, out of the body journeys lead to the concept of the *Aethyr*, or the *30 levels of the astral plane positioned between the physical plane and divinity, which have to be re-ascended through complex techniques of a magical-mystical character.*

At this point we have to consider a further specific faculty: *the sense of dimensions*, or the ability to translate a system of laws into something else. Exercising this faculty means being aware of interacting with many dimensions at the same time and of travelling from one world to another, from one possible dimension to another, just as is part of our nature.
This faculty is indispensible for understanding experiences which are very different from our current perceptions.

Our psycho-physical vehicle is not the 'original model', just as this reality (which derives from it) is not the one originally attributed to our level of complexity. We currently live in much more limited and conventional lines of reality, passing casually from one to another.

Because of this — according to various psychological and metaphysical models— our soul is described as likewise fragmented into diverse and confused personalities, or into many 'I's as was proposed by Gurdjieff. Our soul lacks a complete and unitary sense of the reality that constitutes the scenario of our experience of consciousness and, as a consequence lacks the perception of us as beings that are likewise complete and unitary: it is a vicious circle. But rather than work on the integration of our illusory 'I's (a model that still insists on the separation of ourselves), we have to work on the integration of reality and put the concept we have lost back together again. Our soul is unitary and yet infinitely versatile, so much so it has us believe that we are many souls! It is not the personalities in themselves that are separate and move around inside of us, but it is the fluctuation of our vague and confused perceptions on the lines where we have fragmented reality that induces us to perceive ourselves as similarly confused and fragmented, mind based and deceived.

We have already seen that the major part of our 'unconscious' corresponds to the universe that we do not 'see', because even though we determine it, we are not conscious of the fact nor do we perceive or control it, not being conscious, perceiving or having control of ourselves.

If we let this 'iceberg' emerge, then both reality and our soul personalities would reassemble in a linear and coherent dimensional picture: we need a sense of unity, of 'soul' to be precise, regardless of the current expressions of our fragmented identity.

Leaving aside theories on the structure of the soul, we have to consider the fragmentation of the spirit throughout the dimensions and time like various facets of an essential unity that needs to be retrieved in order to achieve a more authentic sense of ourselves and life.

Such an objective can be pursued with the use of another inner faculty of fundamental importance which results in an awareness of the self: True Will (or the faculty of *Intent*).

The sense of True Will is the quality of knowing how to use the power of your own *True Will*, as Crowley called it, which leads us back to the most authentic part of ourselves, and consciously guides our evolution in harmony with the evolution of everything else.

The 'Will', with the exercise of this sense, becomes the ability to define and direct your own plane of existence, namely your own line of evolutionary reality through the conscious use and power of free will, assisted by a progressive knowledge of the authentic mechanisms by which reality functions.

True Will does not limit itself to the expression of choice, but actively creates events and synchronic opportunities. We have to re-appropriate the power of the Will: not the Will tied to the fickle desires of our illusory identities but the True Will that is moved by our divine identity and its evolutionary project.

However, if to *do*, you need to *be*, then to *will* you need to know what it is you really want, or better still, you need to know who you really are and awaken your True Identity which is hidden behind multiform expressions of the ego.

Consciousness of the Divine Self corresponds to the faculty of being fully aware of one's origins, nature and real essence. Perceiving one's divine essence is an act of profound awareness and 'communion'. It coincides with the shifting of the barycentre of our illusory masks to a more authentic and radical expression of the Self.

Whilst the Will is the sense of evolutionary direction which corresponds to the real mission of our Consciousness immersed in time and the material world, the sense of the Divine – another inner faculty – leads us to the natural perception of everything being a part of ourselves. We are actually talking more about a sense of *participation* than a sense of perception. In fact of communion, of *love*.

Will and love, metaphorically speaking are the vertical and horizontal axes of our divine centre. We can also interpret the equivalent functions of Yoga and Tantra in the same way: the first means 'union', it supplies the sensation of travelling along the vertical axis: the union of the earth with the sky, of the material with the spiritual, of the human self with God. Therefore it represents the evolutionary direction and educates the Will to identify the Principle with the Goal.

However, Tantra, which literally means 'fabric', creates an image of the weft of reality, of communion, sharing, or of the extension of the horizontal axis; that sense of union and participation in all things. Although diversified into differing levels of self-awareness, every material Form contains the same divine nature.

'Feeling' the divine unity in all things means being 'in communion' here and now, just as everywhere and for always. It signifies *to love*.

Of this sense of the divine, which we could even define as *of the sacred* because through it we participate in the sacrality of each and every thing, we all conserve a subtle memory, much, much more so than for other inner faculties. This memory manifests as the yearning of every individual for the transcendent, for the absolute, but also to self-questioning, to asking "Who am I?" It is the inexplicable and precious inquietude which persists even though we have absolved our physical, intellectual and emotional necessities. The sense of the divine puts us in tune with higher forces and values inside and outside of ourselves.

Such inquietude is transformed into evolutionary energy by religion, in the most correct meaning of the word, while historical religions have suppressed, if not exploited that yearning often for very grim ends.

The 'sense of Self' cannot limit itself to awareness and therefore to the mere contemplation of *who it really is*, but must be applied to the reality that we are now called upon to explore, or to our reality which is the evolutionary project of that self same Consciousness. The awareness of Self is completed by *not forgetting* who it is and in the experience of the material world. In fact our experience of being human has to be redirected towards this real identity so that it is not just a vain illusion. This result is achieved through the practice of *remembering the self*, or the immersed Higher Self, which is adapted to and active in our life.

All this corresponds to the magic significance of Memory defined as the awareness of our real identity and our extension *in time*.

Through the reawakening of the *sense of memory* we can perceive our 'temporal body', that is our real and simultaneous extension throughout time: in short all our lives, including those that we generically define as 'previous', which are in fact parallel or even future lives, given that all lives are contemporaneous.

The sense of memory is *awareness* or participation. Each one of us is the sum of all the experiences we have lived and will live, in different forms, in different bodies, in different times and dimensions. We are a 'point of attention' in which everything is PRESENT. We are *a consciousness that incarnated in Time*, even before it incarnated in space and all its possible dimensions.

Rather than talking about reincarnation as a process of reawakening we should call it *reconnection*. Reawakening the *sense of memory* we will certainly recall previous lives but not because we access a mnemonic recording but because we are *living them contemporaneously*: we are the essence that accumulates them and employs them as if they were probes in time and matter. These are our lives, our 'incarnations': the probes, the tentacles of *consciousness* that give shape to us.

We do not access the memories but the awareness of our life, of its real extension, which transcends its current bodily identification in space-time.

From the moment we *remember* who we truly are and perceive our true multi-dimensional body; we can finally identify and determine which line of existence corresponds to our mission. It is from that moment that we determine not only the present and the future of our soul personality but also our previous lives. It is therefore necessary to overcome the definitions and the logic that sustain research into past lives, those processes, including regressive hypnosis, that are not based upon the exploration of ourselves in our current life and from there open up to all the rest as a natural consequence of the Reawakening.

Identify with yourself and feel the real extension of yourself, throughout time and in all dimensions where the consciousness-that-you are, is found simultaneously, in the past, present and future.

There is no difference, there is no distance. That is your 'body', that is your real identity, in which every life is nothing but a sense, a limb, a window on the worlds of the possible that we are here to discover, in order to discover ourselves. Use the breath, use all of the body to feel this expansion and to perceive the new awareness.

Other faculties exist which we can conventionally classify in different ways: from the para-telepathic faculties to those of our clairvoyant mind, from the perceptive sensitivity of our aura to the faculty of the heart as en emotional sensor. When dealing with the faculties linked to highly subjective explorations and personal life experiences, the most valid guide for a more in-depth examination is personal sensitivity.

The Vital Energies

The complete and controlled expression of our inner faculties cannot be omitted from the reintegration of our identity, the harmonious reawakening of our chakra and the correct and aware use of our vital energies.
Almost the entire sum of our vital and spiritual energies originates in the sexual sphere (a much broader concept than simply 'having sex'). The sexual energy that I am referring to can express itself directly or indirectly in forms that are more or less controlled and harmonious.

The *indirect* expression of sexual energy includes all our creative expressions, above all artistic ones, but also expresses itself in relationships which draw on sexual energy as a source.

The *direct* expression of sexuality, from an esoteric point of view, distinguishes itself for the most part in an active *humid path*[17] and a contained *dry path*[18].

---

[17] As far as this is concerned on the ritual-operational plane we talk about Sexual Magic, while on the more mystical plane we use the term Tantra.
[18] Various forms of monastic life.

There are different spiritual and operational magic traditions - setting aside evaluations of a moralistic kind, for freely and consciously experimenting – always in the sphere of tradition and magic-mystic discipline – with different forms of individual sexuality, be they hetero/homosexual or in plural contexts, which in turn follow different formulas.

In the context of such traditions, the mature and aware individual is considered free to relate or not, to any partner on any level, thus completely transcending sexuality by fully living it or sublimating it.

Sexual Magic is the most important aspect of the Alchemy of Living Forces.

The energy can be directed inside oneself (for example to reawaken the chakra or Kundalini or to achieve an androgynous state) and outside the self, to create and nourish thought forms or entities, or even to act upon events and synchronicity according to very complex formulas.

The directing of sexual energies is a magical and spiritual possibility of great importance because it corresponds to the conscious use of the great energetic potential that is contained inside each and every one of us.

However, it is important to remember that we are talking about an alchemical discipline that requires seriousness, maturity and elevation in the way that it is lived, not only in terms of sexual relationships but also as regards the emotions and feelings involved. Only in this way can our sexuality, whether it is expressed or contained, be consciously directed towards a spiritual reawakening, the completion of the self, magic, theurgic and generative alchemical operations or the reawakening of subtle, spiritual energies and faculties. These forces, that we nevertheless express in our ordinary lives (even though in an unconscious and casual form), have to be used in a constructive way, or else they suffer from the limits of our conditioning and our more base and egoistic instincts, transforming themselves into deformities of the mind, obsessions and parasitic entities.

In Tantra the realization of the androgen happens through the relationship with a partner, in the context of a relationship that is elevated to priestly dignity (ierogamìa): in woman, man finds a reflection of his own feminine aspects, just as woman finds a point of reference in man to reawaken her masculine aspects. These are operations that above all demand that indispensible premise, the full recovery of ones femininity and masculinity in line with ones current psycho-physical nature, its functions and most authentic virtues. A nature that is often (think of the conditions of women), profoundly repressed or perverted.

In European culture the figure of the androgen first appears in Plato's description in the 'Symposium': in the dialogue, Aristophanes speaks of this third gender, not as a child of the Sun like men, nor a daughter of the Earth like women, but as a son of the Moon, which the nature of both participate in. The myth says that self-sufficient completeness makes androgynous humans arrogant enough to imagine they can scale Mount Olympus, and Zeus (not wanting to destroy them and deprive Olympus of their sacrifices), divides each one in half, reducing them to just masculine and feminine.

That which Elémire Zolla calls the never placated 'human nostalgia for wholeness', is the root and in someway the constraint on love (« to the brama and to the pursuit of wholeness, well, touches the name of love»). In Hindu metaphysics, the masculine polarity represented by Śiva (the destroyer) and that of the feminine represented by Shakti (Parvati, the divine energy), need *Ardhanarishvara*, or the androgen in order to fuse together.

In the West's platonic narration, the androgen's persistence and its use in successive culture, such as alchemy, signal the archetype of the *'coincidentia oppositorum'* in the androgen. Nourished by Neo-Platonism and alchemical studies, the men of Humanism and the Renaissance turned the figure of the androgen into one of great importance.

The modern image of the androgen aims for completeness and integration, not only on the religious and mystic plane but also on the psychological plane and in terms of image. Such completeness also implies, apart from the integration of essences on alchemical and metaphysical planes, an integration of the perception of the world. This is achieved thanks to the contemporaneous and complete employment of the right and left hemispheres of the brain, that is: rational-masculine processing and intuitive feminine processing. A heightened awareness of our own profound dimensions can then be celebrated along with an integration of the individual personalities of the soul structure.

In certain tantric traditions, but also in those of the Middle East, it is not taken for granted that a man will express his masculine aspect in a predominant manner or that a woman will express her feminine aspect; this does not detract from masculinity or femininity and the value of heterosexual relationships. Theories exist however, in which the rediscovery or the completion of our complementary aspect does not necessarily have to correspond to relations with the opposite sex: it is worth saying that the completion can also occur between individuals of the same sex.

The androgen would be a forewarning of the so-called Alchemical Nuptials: the union of our human aspect with that of the divine.

During sexual relations, at the moment of union, a moment of 'presence' can be experienced, an instant in which one intuits a sense of completeness, during which cosmic and divine energies may flow. According to certain schools of thought, the practice of Sexual Magic can be used to achieve a special physical conception. It is employed, in fact, in operations to *program incarnations*, or to encourage the incarnation of selected and evolved souls in the body of the unborn baby (Avatar Magic) also, directly or indirectly, by means of alien or higher entities.

The 'dry path' could be more appropriately considered as the containment or sublimation of sexual expression. The monk, male or female, from an esoteric point of view, has the task of directing their energies through abstinence: the monk aims for the same objectives of spiritual realization and the completion of the self but this does not happen by means of 'the other' but through an individual process that is personally guided and or exclusively directed towards higher forces or ideals. Historically many Orders of Knights assumed a monastic investiture to best express their role as defenders or pursue sacred values.

In many Orders a 'short-term' or temporary monastic period is practiced in which certain rules typical of monastic life are observed, for example: celibacy, prayer, a vegetarian diet and so on. Often it is a period of reflection and spiritual retreat, or a phase of preparation before assuming a special role in an initiatory context.

From an esoteric point of view, the permanent couple - exclusive and stable – and the path of abstinence correspond to precise sacred pathways, in as much as they are very extraordinary choices, especially if the contract is intended for an indeterminate amount of time (something that is rarely encountered in the esoteric field). Besides being an authentic sacred pathway, such choices are considered dangerous because – if not channelled by conscious motivation and discipline – they can lead to repressive and restrictive implications that consequently deform human nature[19].

A path of inner search does not have to - and certainly not straightaway - focus on Tantra and sexual magic. They are complex and difficult themes to deal with if the mind has not first been purified of moral taboo and the malice that ensues.

Greatly welcomed however are moments of personal reflection on this theme, with a partner and later perhaps in a group context, with psychological and meta-psychological support, to open the mind and heart to greater equilibrium. It goes without saying that all of this requires great maturity and purity of mind.

Whether or not, we feel inclined towards this Path or particular need, one that many consider a 'minefield', in the deepening of our inner relationship with the Self, it must be said that a

---

[19] In effect, even though commonly accepted (opportunely conditioned by the seats of socio-political and religious powers with the aim of controlling and subjugating), the formula of the couple united in holy matrimony, just as that of priestly celibacy, can often result in hypocrisy and psychological problems or even dangerous perversion.

healthy or serene sex life, that is free but most of all aware, is the basis for an overall harmony that certainly renders the examination, the emancipation, and the expression of the Higher Self, smoother and more effective.

Even though I do not want to enter too much into the merit of traditions and practices for reawakening and consciously managing sexual energies, it is useful at this point to say a couple of words about the so called 'Left-hand way or path'.

Tantrism and the Left-hand Path

In the Hindu tradition, while the word Yoga means 'Union' – with one's own soul, the cosmos, with God – and includes many different techniques of a physical, mental and spiritual kind (to achieve awareness, meditation, devotion, conscious action, and the truth), Tantra means 'Loom', or also 'thread', 'continuity' and communion. Tantrism consists of many esoteric traditions of Hinduism and Buddhist philosophy and is considered a sort of 'short cut' to the full Realization of Consciousness, Enlightenment.

In Tantra we distinguish between two principal paths: the 'dakshinachara' (or 'samayachara'), the Right-hand Path, and the 'vamachara' (or 'vamamarg'), the Left-hand Path. These terms were adopted and abundantly used by Western occultists, often in the wrong way or distorted by a hinterland of Catholic moralism.

Tantra, in all its different possible expressions, is not to be seen as Vedic tradition. The rituals of the Tantric Left-hand path, in particular, are often rejected or considered extremely dangerous by orthodox Hinduism. However, in Tibetan

Buddhism, Tantrism plays a central role and is totally harmonized with Yoga thanks to the Buddhist code whose ethics mitigate the most dangerous aspects of tantric practices.

Certain practitioners search for the union of masculine and feminine principles inside themselves, through paths of sublimation and union with spiritual forces. In other cases the union, or rather the completion, comes through sexual practices, during which the divine union of Shiva and Shakti is celebrated. In tantric practice Mantra (formulas), Yantra (vehicles) and Mandala (patterns) are also used. Sexual practices carried out in a ritual form are not only an aspect of tantric alchemy but are without doubt central to *Vama-marg* Orders.

The conscious management of sexual energy is the basic element in this practice and there is quite a distinction between working *white* and working *black*.

In white work, the energy, in order to be directed towards the reawakening of higher consciousness cannot be discharged by ejaculation while in black work it is achieved through the completion of the sexual act.

In the first case we have a form of separation from desire, in the second its exaltation. In each case the sacred objective remains the same, though neither path is exempt from all kinds of deviance when not sustained by the necessary knowledge and spiritual maturity.
The most important Tantric Schools are the *Kaula* and *Vamachara* Circles.

In the West Tantra has been assimilated as the use of sexuality in the context of magic (or mystical) experiences and appears in many different operative and theoretical formulas. For example, what we can learn about Tantra from Crowley, Grant, Reich or Osho, may appear very different and yet the various approaches can and should be reconciled, given that they are all complimentary depending on their path.

The Right-hand Path and the Left-hand Path are two different approaches to achieving the same result. Generically, the Right-hand Path concentrates on the observance of a precise code of ethics, morals and devotion towards one or more divinities, while the Left-hand Path pursues the exploration and evolution of the Self before any other objective.

All in all, from the Thelemic and neo-Gnostic point of view, it is a false dichotomy but one which indicates two very different paths. The second path, with its emphasis on the Super-Conscious Self, has often meant and been wrongly considered as egoistic, therefore associated with 'Satanism' or 'black magic': the devil, evil, the dark, evil portents, hell and to the overwhelming power of the feminine, that power which has to be – as the sad story of the Inquisition teaches us – subordinated and condemned. Such moral condemnation originates not only in the influence of Judaic-Christian patriarchy and the reactionary culture of Catholicism – and more recently from a certain syncretistic 'gnosis' which is rather pretentious abstruse and bigoted – but also from inside the same esoteric movements. This often occurs in a contradictory way as in the case of Blavatsky who described certain practices as immoral, even though in certain of her lesser known works (for example in the magazine *Lucifer*), she does not refrain from considering certain magic–mystical aspects of the tantric-sexual tradition of the East. Also Crowley, when he refers to the 'Black Brothers' speaks of the Brothers of the Left-hand Path, but with a very different meaning, referring to those who have failed and who have not gone beyond the enticements of the ego. Those whose presumption rather than leading them to Genius, has lead them to Madness and a loss of control, who are engulfed by the profound forces within that they themselves have reawakened. When confronting the Abyss they then do not know how to offer all of themselves in order to be reborn as shinning Stars (image of the Higher Self).

The Left-hand Path is considered as the most direct and rapid path to enlightenment but it is also the most dangerous, given the unexpected potential expressed by the energies involved and reawakened.

Today it is often referred to as the Draconian, *Qliphotic* or Dark Path of the Kabbalistic Tree although in this case, there are also many different methods and schools of thought.

The *Magick* of Crowley integrates the two paths into a complete magical-mystical process without placing too much emphasis on their distinction unlike the work of Kenneth Grant which clearly highlights the differences.

A Spiritual Approach to Healing and Well-being

Our biological body is the most complete alchemical laboratory in existence. The human being is able to synthesize thousands of substances in its body. Each element corresponds to a precise process that involves physical, emotive, subtle and spiritual aspects. A complex relationship exists between physical organs, vital energies, the *senses* and the different essences that comprise our soul. Every part of the human being is essential to all others and each one is at the centre of a complex network of physical, mental and spiritual correspondences. Not only can we ideally be the Master of ourselves but we can also be Healers of our own body.

Natural medicine, in fact, with the aim of re-establishing the indispensible equilibrium for the conservation of health and well-being, considers that treating the individual in his or her entirety and in relation to the environment, produces a better result than merely treating the body as the simple sum of its parts. This approach is defined as 'holistic'

According to traditional concepts, disease originates from an energetic imbalance caused by different factors: such lack of balance has repercussions on the psychic and nervous spheres and results in influencing the physical.

From a spiritual point of view – but also psychological - a limited and confused awareness of ourselves and our bodies is already a kind of 'disease'.

The body and the spirit are part of the same reality. Therefore disease in general terms, putting aside that which is severe, the result of particular circumstances, or of an extraordinary character – is ideally seen as a sign of imbalance and a lack of

106

inner harmony. We can think of disease as the synchronic voice of our 'inner master' who provokes us to reflect on ourselves, our lives and values: the process of real healing therefore corresponds to a process of *comprehension* and personal growth.

According to traditions of 'spiritual healing' by 'channelling Prana' it is possible to re-establish the equilibrium that is indispensable to the conservation of health and well-being. According to spiritual traditions *Prana* arrives directly from the cosmos, from the sources of life: it is the archetype of well-being, the matrix of health. It corresponds to a state of vital, intelligent dynamic balance that can be simply identified with the ideal concepts of well-being and 'feeling good', without limiting the concept to a *lack of disease* but referring to it as a more complete sense of realization. Feeling 'well' in fact does not simply mean 'not being ill' but rather, attaining that cognitive, creative and spiritual potential inherent in human nature.

Prana is an energy that the healer channels in an 'indifferent' way, without using conjecture, the mind, or personal energy to interfere and without activating any personal capacity to heal, be it real or presumed.

The concept of 'well-being' – and the relative intervention – is more about prevention than therapy: the attention is all on the person, on life, on the expansion of well-being and not on the illness as such. Once having manifested, the illness requires suitable therapeutic measures, as non-invasive as possible, which take into account the type, urgency and severity of each case and the means that are available.

An intelligent integration of cures produces the maximum effect. The 'healer' in the guise of a mere 'therapist', which he is not really, should work in tandem with the doctor without disturbing the situation so that the process of healing can perfect itself because of the 'upstream' energetic intervention. In this way the disease does not reappear in different ways or places but is completely resolved.

The healer must not be a therapist but rather the 'facilitator' of a reawakening of consciousness, in which the client must be the responsible protagonist. A new found well-being cannot help but manifest as the natural consequence of this very radical process.

The work of the prana-therapist has therefore to be carried out in such a context and not end up in the plagiarism of diagnostic procedures and conventional medicine. Otherwise it risks only distinguishing itself in terms of the forms and instruments it uses and not from the concept. A concept which is focused on the organ, the symptom and the disease and therefore confirms an approach and therapeutic intervention that is basically physical (although working with bio-psycho-energetic instruments), rather than holistic.

The 'healer' – in a shamanic sense and I stand by my argument – is above all a bearer of Consciousness, who is also involved in a pathway of personal spiritual growth and is consequently able to help others to regain a state of harmony and conserve it. The healer acts on a spiritual, energetic and subtle plane, mostly preventative and eventually integrated and complementary, in perfect harmony with conventional therapeutic procedures. He/she does not enter into the merit of the diagnosis, or comment on the frame of mind of the doctor, or offer to specifically cure an illness, which could just be resolved through the natural consequences of a broader consciousness of the self.

This kind of 'healer' does not transmit their own vital energy, but channels the *universal energy*, to encourage a process of Consciousness: the conscious reawakening *in the person* of their own energies, of their sense of responsibility, of their 'inner healer'. It is the process of understanding the self which is true growth and which leads to the well-being of mind, body and spirit. A process that the healer also has to constantly undergo by working on his/herself.

Being a 'healer' means becoming a channel for vital energies (*Prana*) to encourage harmony, vigour and health in oneself and others. 'Pranic' energy, or an ideal model of universal balance and holistic well-being, is called upon and projected without using instruments or equipment of any kind, just oneself as a living bearer of energy and well-being.

The Sanskrit term *Prana* literally means *life*, and was later seen as breath. It is the archetype of health or better still of existential equilibrium and harmony.

The *channelling of Prana* therefore does not envisage a diagnosis and does not consist of a specific therapy. It is the *flow of vital energy*, which through resonance enables the existential equilibriums that preside over the well-being and evolution of mind, body and spirit 'upstream', to be maintained (or to re-establish) themselves.

It is important to remember that the aim is to prevent and not to cure, although applications of Prana can, if necessary, be harmonized with all kinds of therapeutic procedures. In such cases the objective is to 'reawaken the healer' that each of us has inside and foster a holistic process of understanding, the betterment of life, the relationship with oneself, surrounding reality and others.

Ideally the person is rendered autonomous and in turn becomes a *Prana channel* by learning and adopting certain meditation and breathing techniques.

In shamanic tradition the *medicine-man* sustains and transmits his 'power' by extolling his personal charisma, with the help of suggestions and expedients. In Africa, I personally attended some very bizarre methods practiced by a tribe of the Cameroon; afterwards the sorcerer confided his real opinion about the phenomenon of healing to me, describing it as a phenomenon of consciousness: "The healer always lives inside of you, and in each case indirectly triggers a process of understanding in the person who is ill: this is what really happens, all the rest is just theatre".
And even more interesting from the point of view of our metaphysics is the spiritual concept of 'reconnection' when applied to therapy. By removing the causes behind the disease the person moves to a new line of reality which also modifies the past: in this way, it is not that a person is 'healed' but rather that they move to a new line of existence in which they were never ill in the first place.

The Structure and Evolution of the Human Soul

What follows is a structural model that originates in many hypotheses, conceptions and conjecture on the human soul, evolution, the dynamics of death and reincarnation and on our transcendent and immanent nature. It is a perspective that can be looked at in more depth and applied to many fields, from avant-garde *transpersonal psychology* to speculations of a more theoretical, religious and esoteric kind, all of which have some interesting and significant ideas to offer.

The basic concepts are to be found scattered throughout many traditions - from Hasidism[20] to Buddhism – and in the studies and analyses of many researchers and Masters who have frequently insisted on the complexity of our spiritual and existential nature. It is made up of psychological elements as well as those intrinsic to our nature as pluri-dimensional beings, as individuals who are searching for a lost spiritual integrity and striving to recover and develop a unitary and definitively authentic awareness of reality.
Among these researchers Aurobindo, Gurdjieff and Crowley particularly stand out. In his esoteric novel, 'The Moonchild'[21] Crowley gives us a meaningful description of the phenomenon which I will be developing further here.

Having considered the hypothesis of our 'fragmentedness', or better still the fragmented representation that we have of

---

[20] Hasidism is a Hebrew faction founded by Baal Shem Tov in the XVIII century.
[21] Aleister Crowley, *The Moonchild*, 1917, Chapter II.

reality and ourselves, we can focus on the fundamental integrity and uniqueness of our consciousness and on the re-assembly of our different parts. We need to consider our uniqueness as natural and the current conditions of loss, fragmentation and conflict as the result of a path gone astray, of an unnatural illusion, but one which nevertheless has to be our point of departure.

We can basically confirm that the human being has three fundamental natures or converging states which constitute its microcosm:

1. Physical body
2. Soul
3. Spiritual essence

Each of these *bodies* possesses a complex and organic structure: the *physical body* with its organs and apparatus, the *soul* with its multi-form expressions coloured by the divine spark in evolution and the profound *spiritual component* that relates the Microcosm to the Macrocosm (*as above so below*). The objective is to acquire full consciousness of these three bodies and of the existential dimensions related to them.

In the following table we can see this triadic principle according to different perspectives:

Number	Reality	Form	Individual	Alchemy	Gunas
3	Form	Matter/Energy	Body	Salt	Tamas
2	Threshold	Complexity	Soul Structure	Mercury	Rajas
1	Real	Attractor/Intelligence	Spirit/Being	Sulphur	Sattva

Vedanta	Judaism	Hermeticism	Sources	Deities	Endoteric Path
Jagrat/Manas	Nepesh	Soma/Physis	Energy	Son/Daughter	Social Aspect
Jiva-Atman	Ruach	Psyche/Pneuma	Knowledge/Memory	Mother	Explorative Aspect
Brahman	Neshamah	Nous/Pleroma	Power/Will	Father	Mystic Aspect

The three natures converge and define the individual in all its aspects, physical, subtle and spiritual. They are coordinated by the *chakra* which act as interfaces to the various states, refining and modulating the different spiritual, subtle and vital energies that are indispensable to existence.

The Structure of the Individual Soul

I do not know who I am, what soul I have. When I speak with sincerity, I do not know with what sincerity I speak. I am varyingly other than the I that I am not sure exists (or if it is that of others). I feel faith that I do not have. I feel multiple...plural like the universe... I feel I am living other people's lives, in me, incompletely, in a sum of non – I s synthesized into a false I.

Fernando Pessoa

Let's begin with this idea: the soul of each one of us is a complex and fragmented structure just as our perception of reality is complex and fragmented.

113

Aurobindo, Yogananda, Steiner, Bailey, Crowley, Gurdjieff, Jung, Krishnamurti, Raphael, Castaneda and Osho are perhaps the most quoted authorities on modern mystical-magic research. They have all confirmed and insisted on the necessary re-integration of the self and of a more coherent perception of reality, as an indispensable starting point for every successive evolutionary pretension.

The basic concept can be found in the fact that having lost consciousness of reality, which is much vaster than that which we currently perceive; we fluctuate confusedly between disassociated conventional states. These states are illusory and determine our likewise conventional, disassociated and illusory identity.

We fluctuate between different and always vague lines of an elusive reality, having lost our more powerful original completeness. A wholeness, which is longer-lived, broader and less dense in respect to the 'impulsiveness' that makes up our body in this impenetrable and fictitious reality[22]. And on these lines of reality parts of us are shattered and scattered, emerging in the course of life as diversified expressions of a confused identity, simply as a result of the casual fluctuation from one illusion to another and from one line to another[23]. But we do not have an inkling of it: it would seem that 'here inside' this 'body' there are different and disassociated personalities, in life as in death each one with its desires, character, whims and reasoning.

---

[22] In the process of recomposing reality like ourselves our psycho-physical vehicle will also probably change, perhaps recovering a more etheric and less material like state.

[23] The concept was admirably taken up by Vadim Zeland in his theory of 'Reality Transurfing'.

We are an incoherent and inconclusive collection of pseudo-lives caught up in the vicious circle of *Samsara* (cycle of incarnations). Asleep in our diving suits always calling 'I' that which confusedly surfaces, deluding ourselves that it is a real and consistent identity even though we are aware of our inner conflicts and apprehensions. And we continue to call the illusion of the moment *reality* just as we continue to call the personality of the moment *'I'*.

This is how from a certain point of view the many 'packets of experience', that we could define as 'individual personalities', distinguish themselves in a physical body: the developing experiences constitute a coherent structure which is incarnated in the same body, aggregated and organized in such a way as to allow the various parts to express themselves and even potentially to evolve.

Science, too, is beginning to discover that in various abnormal circumstances; totally different personalities may chase each other through a single body. [...] and how, indeed, half - a-dozen personalities could take turns to live in one body. That they are real independent souls is shown by the fact that not only do the contents of the mind differ – which might conceivably be fake but their handwritings, their voices, and that in ways which are quite beyond anything we know in the way of conscious simulation, or even possible simulation.

Aleister Crowley – The Moonchild

Today, because of how we are made and because of how we perceive – in fact as a result of particular effects that we vaguely ascertain – we can theorize that many 'individuals' make up the complex physical-spiritual structure which is adapted to the 'psycho-physical vehicle' (our body); the consciousness of which is organized by mechanisms of awareness that are more or less evolved. The various parts are allowed to express themselves, to perceive and participate in some form of reality and therefore potentially evolve.

According to esoteric traditions, the structure of the soul begins to incarnate a short time before birth, to complete itself – like a sort of housing ready to be filled with human experiences – around seventy days later[24], with the first development of that experiential receptacle that we define as the *'personality in formation'*.

In fact alongside the 'personalities' that come together at birth (imagined as packets of experience that reincarnate to complete themselves), that originate from a more or less coherent formative path (other lives) an additional new developing identity or *personality in formation* is generated which refers to and represents the current existential identity and its specific meanings: the point of aggregation and *the representative 'I' of the current experiential status.* As far as we are concerned we are talking about our present life, the one we are 'conscious' of now.

Each individual soul is therefore a coherent structure basically composed of two parts:

1. A combination of personalities (or the soul considered as separated into different personalities that come together in the current identity or in a coherent global identity with regard to its formative path distributed through time).

---

[24] Just as after physical death the soul takes around seventy days to definitively leave the material plane.

2. A catalyzing element that, in the jargon of esoteric physics, is defined as the *attractor*, which constitutes the profound essence of our nature in as much as it is part of the All. It is the aggregate spiritual essence that assembles the different parts, including the *personality in formation* which is specific to a particular incarnation. The attractor is what we commonly define as 'spirit': an aspect of the Real, *an absolute principle of intelligence* which is equal in every individual (according to Hebrew tradition we have a psycho-physical body, *Nefesh-Guph*, the soul - the *Ruach*, and the spirit - the *Neschamah*).

It is called the 'attractor' in esoteric physics jargon because one imagines it attracting personalities to itself according to criteria of perfect reciprocal compatibility and evolutionary potential. The attractor is a principle of absolute *intelligence* in as much as it is an aspect of the Real that permeates every material Form. In fact, if in the transcendent the Real is *Absolute Truth*, its expression in immanence, fragmented into multiple relations between growing *parts*, it expresses itself as *intelligence*. We no longer have ONE absolute reference but the absolute capacity to process the multiple and changing *partial truths* that relate to one another and verge upon that ONE.

According to this *'Theory of The Personalities'* the attractor, at the moment in which the soul structure is formed, just before the birth, attracts and assembles those individualities which are still incomplete in respect to their potential evolution (as if they were 'amounts' of experience) and which could represent the perfect synergic integration of a 'wining team' capable of deriving the best evolutionary result from the current incarnation, not just as a result of each individual but as a synthetic result; a new distillation.

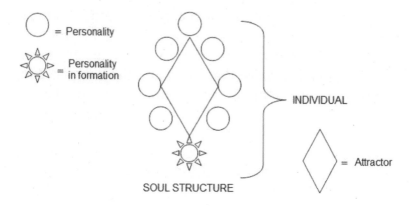

O = Personality

Personality in formation

INDIVIDUAL

= Attractor

SOUL STRUCTURE

Nevertheless – let's not forget – we are always *uniquely* 'us' but because we participate in a fractional and discontinuous reality in space and time, our real identity is perceived and described as fragmented (and consequently in practice becomes so) in space as in time, even though it continues to be the head of a unique central spiritual essence. I say 'in time' because our incarnations are also nothing more than a limited perception of our simultaneous extensions as higher consciousness in dimensions of the possible. Just as our inner personalities are fragments of a central and immanent unity, in the same way our incarnations are nothing more than the fragmented perceptions of our transcendent identity.

The Counter-attractor

Another aspect worth mentioning, even though rather disturbing and the subject of a more in-depth analysis of those 'Dark Paths' (such as the Tiphonian Orders, the paths of the Qliphotic Kabbalah and Chaos Magick) that are certainly not easy to follow or describe, is that of the 'Counter-attractor' or the door on the *counter-universe* (*Da'at*) from which the compensatory forces of existence flow, the inertia that opposes life and evolution through a degenerative resistance on the psycho-physical and spiritual plane.

In spite of being negative, the 'counter-attractor' is also part of the great game of equilibrium and polarity but at a much higher level than the play of forces we normally refer to when we talk about positive and negative, good and evil, light and dark, yin and yang. It is thanks to the counter-attractor that the existent is able to affirm the phenomenon of Absolute Consciousness.

The Divine Spark and Free Will

We can define the 'Divine Spark' (*Yechidah*), as a fragment of the Primeval Divinity (*Zureh*) which is an active element of evolved species with a sufficient level of *complexity*. The *active* role of the divine spark depends on a natural process in which, having reached a determined level of structural complexity, a material Form 'ascends' and becomes an active expression of the development of Consciousness in the Universe. We could imagine that the divine spark magnetizes the various personalities around the *attractor* and establishes itself in each one.

In an incarnated soul structure it forms that *divine principle* which is potentially self-conscious and the bearer of free will. It is capable of self-perception, which is what distinguishes a 'bridge-Form' from other material Form.

It is important to remember that free will not only refers to the physical aspects of existence. Consciousness (God) distinguishes the world up to predetermined borders: Nature has its own laws just as the dynamics of our mind and body have their precise functions and in the same way define new conditions and social conventions.

What does free will consist of inside these preordained mechanisms?

Free will does not originate from divine, natural or social mechanisms; it refers to the 'person', to the added value that everyone produces and represents in terms of their own identity: that which goes beyond mere physicality to construct a higher and refined consciousness.

The Fragmentation of Reality and the Bridge-Form

This reality of ours not only appears fragmented but each one of us has fallen into the density of a *mental materialism* which is heavy, opaque and inconsistent.

The fall does not mean that our lives sink, they act like probes in existence at different depths (dimensions) but rather, that we lose consciousness of the *real self* which happened 'upstream'. Our unique identity is consequently disassociated in space and time and then perceived as fragmented into illusory identities and separate *incarnations*. Identities which are briefly sketched by a temporal mind, one that transforms us into beings that are divided and unaware even of our current reality, leaving us engrossed in psycho-physical dimensions that are all fictitious.

We live on a conventional plane of existence, the result of an approximated and continually reprocessed average of lines of reality on which we fluctuate chaotically, in a space of variables that are out of control and which our consciousness nevertheless tries to organize logically. We move onto the lines of reality that 'serve us' most, even though we only have a conventional perception of them.

The average of our fluctuations, collectively established, is what we normally call 'history': the so called *principal plane of existence*, which in itself does not exist, if not as a mental *matrix* held together by an electromagnetic field.

Reality is divided into planes of mental existence (and therefore material) which results in the fragmentation of our soul's personalities: it is a temporal existential and structural disassociation.

We are all profoundly hypnotized by an unreal and inconclusive suggestion: for further thoughts on this subject I advise *The Fall into Time* by the Romanian philosopher E.M. Cioran and for lighter reading *Hypnotizing Maria* by Richard Bach.

Salvation and perdition require the same waste of energy. Losing himself in it demonstrates that, predisposed to failure, he had enough strength to flee, a condition though of refusing growth's manoeuvres. But having no sooner understood the seduction, he abandons himself to it and is stunned: a state of grace based on inebriation that only the approval of unreality dispenses. Everything that is then engaged upon, participates in the inurnment of the insubstantial, of the acquired illusion and the habit of considering existence that which it is not.

121

Specialized in appearances, exercised on the merest trifle (on what and with what else could he ever satisfy his thirst for dominion?), he accumulates knowledge that is but a reflection, true knowledge is not possessed at all: given that his false Science, the reproduction of his false innocence, distracts him from the absolute; all that he knows is not worth knowing.

Fall into Time – E. M. Cioran

Form that carry the divine spark and all the particular spiritual attributes relating to it (including *free will*), take the name 'bridge-Form' in that they have reached a certain level of biological and perceptive complexity. They are assigned the task of mediating human and spiritual existential significance. Reintegrating and transubstantiating this material and biological reality into the sphere of the divine and in the final analysis, into the Real.

In spite of everything, on this planet the current human species is a bridge-Form. Below a certain level of complexity, *divinity* participates in material Form as a passive and not self-aware aspect, even though it is immanent and present in everything and catalyzed by the principle of the Real (attractor) which is in all things[25]. Up to that level, the divine aspect inserted in all things is lead towards evolution, not by virtue of consciousness

---

[25] The mathematician and epistemologist Alfred North Whitehead indicated that there are 'chaos attractors' in everything, thanks to which every process can be linked to every other, simply because all processes are part of the One. After Whitehead, excellent thinkers such as Ilya Prigogine and Erich Jantsch developed new creative principles, that bring to light a reality that is open on many levels, set out in the direction of complexity and articulated in parallel worlds and spiralling temporal structures, consisting of compartmentalized eras, organized on fractal scales, in which the laws are continuously different from one another.

but through the mechanism of universal laws (it is always us who little by little codify at ever increasing levels of complexity up to the divinization of the universe itself!). The attractor (*in us and in all things*) is the natural engine of this mechanism until that level of potential awareness that we call the *divine spark* takes on consciousness: in that moment *Universal intelligence* passes from being the prerogative of the self-referencing attractor (the spirit), to being the manifestation of Consciousness in the material world.

In practice, when a Form manifests that has the capacity to interact at a suitable level with reality – enough to represent the right kind of vehicle for an active consciousness – the immanent divine component (therefore present and having grown by acquiring the mechanisms up to that level of material Form), 'ascends' and begins to actively involve itself in the nature of things and events. Consciously experimenting with distributed immanence, it extricates itself from the labyrinth of *choices* and the multiple interrelated Form of the material world, to get to know itself again, in the *otherness* and *diversity* and in fact give itself a motive to re-evolve. *Free will* is born[26] and therefore so is doubt and choice.

---

[26] At this point we will not stop to consider how much this will can be freely exercised today, conditioned as it is by a myriad of influences and restrictions that are instinctive, environmental, educative and mental etc... For now let's just consider it an aspect that is nevertheless an inexorable part of our nature.

123

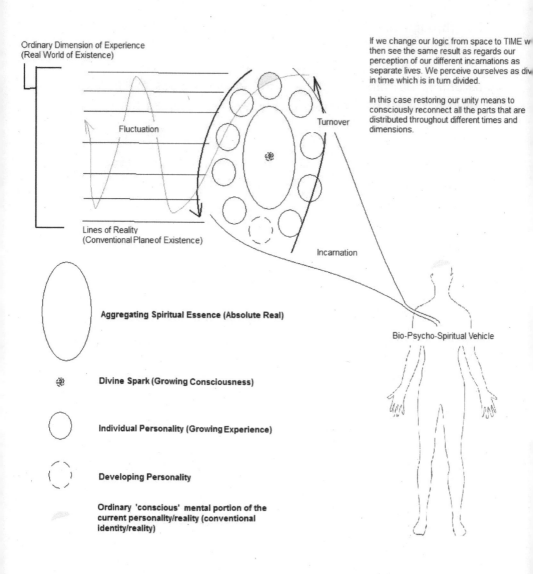

Ordinary Dimension of Experience
(Real World of Existence)

If we change our logic from space to TIME w
then see the same result as regards our
perception of our different incarnations as
separate lives. We perceive ourselves as div
in time which is in turn divided.

In this case restoring our unity means to
consciously reconnect all the parts that are
distributed throughout different times and
dimensions.

Fluctuation

Turnover

Lines of Reality
(Conventional Plane of Existence)

Incarnation

Bio-Psycho-Spiritual Vehicle

Aggregating Spiritual Essence (Absolute Real)

Divine Spark (Growing Consciousness)

Individual Personality (Growing Experience)

Developing Personality

Ordinary 'conscious' mental portion of the
current personality/reality (conventional
identity/reality)

Free will is a double- edged sword. In effect, up to that moment
Form can do nothing but obey the laws of its own nature, but
now in virtue of its exercisable power – given the complexity
achieved and the active intervention of immanent divine power

124

– it enters into the dynamics of awareness, of choice, and therefore the possibility of making mistakes.

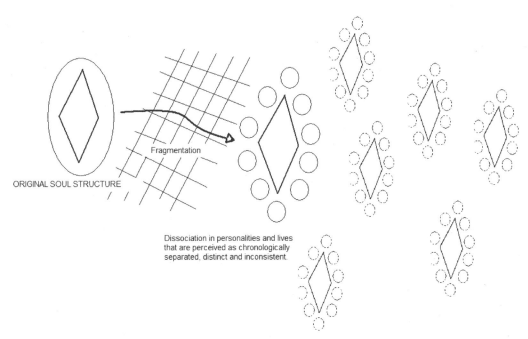

ORIGINAL SOUL STRUCTURE

Fragmentation

Dissociation in personalities and lives that are perceived as chronologically separated, distinct and inconsistent.

Through the personality the divine aspect participates in the dynamics of material Form, until complete Consciousness is achieved in it, or else until its annihilation.

Our soul personalities are the *senses* of the inner divinity, the senses of our real identity and our *emotions* are the perceptions of those senses. This is why we as human beings have to become divinities, gods (or fragments of God) and reunite with our origins by exploring humanity through this possible Universe. Not to transcend this material reality, but to *transubstantiate* it!

The evolution of mankind is more than anything else, the evolution of its consciousness and can be considered as the development in it of those powers and possibilities that we can never develop in a mechanical way but are the consequence of the exercise of its will and conscious actions.

The soul is the vivification of the divine spark in this reality through the power of free will. Spiritual evolution is an extraordinary act activated by the exercise of the Will (*Chiah*).

The reawakening of the Inner God cannot be the consequence of an automatic mechanism but of a growing awareness of the nature of this reality and the capacity to evolve through making the 'right choices'.

If the flesh came into being because of the spirit, it is a wonder. But if the spirit came into being because of the body, it is a wonder of wonders. Indeed I am amazed at how this great wealth has made its home in this poverty.

From The Gospel of Thomas

We are not human beings that have to become 'gods', but gods that intend to become human beings in this 'reflection of Reality' that we call existence. By 'gods' we mean the ideal identity of the truest and most intimate nature of the individual.

To travel the paths of the Universe, God, the Numen, has desperate need of Mankind. Only Mankind can guarantee the integration, the closure of the circle.
Without the consciousness of the human being God cannot become conscious of itself and in turn Mankind cannot complete its existence without becoming conscious of the All[27].

---

[27] Some time ago I read these phrases in a small book but I do not remember its title or even the author: If you know where they are to be found please let me know, thank you.

126

Nevertheless, even though *in pectore* we are gods and we are 'conscious', in effect we are not really so until we have rediscovered that we are and until we have reconstructed our real identity by means of our human life. For this reason the soul, although potentially divine, atrophies, disperses or becomes the object of prey on the part of other forces or species – apart from our mental obsessions. The divine spark is there if it works and works if it serves: and it serves only if the individual proposes objectives and ideals which go beyond the self. Otherwise the individual is nothing more than a 'piece of meat': one that is heavy or light.

It is this that is the real process of the divine nature of our being and it is profoundly in line with evolutionary necessity. Often religions, just as certain schools of thought, tend to recognize in an 'external being' (transcendent or alien – often creating it and therefore subjecting an unaware Mankind to this self same entity!) the power to praise or castigate, judge or save, assign or remove the divine spark from the human species. This subtracts the human being's intrinsic divine authority and subjects it to an arbitrary judgement of 'something else' in respect to the natural parameters of evolution which are its real identity and spiritual commitment.

The Formation of the Personality

Every Form contains the totality of the Universe. Every part is a vehicle for the constituent laws of the whole and it is only through the filter of the senses that such Form manifests in its distinctive identity, just as through the filter of our mind we articulate a sense for reading events: growth.

Be it a simple stone or a more complex organic body, everything is nevertheless a receptacle of a spiritual principle. On every scale, every kind of manifestation consists of a *physical* structure (mass/energy/time), of a soul structure (in which increasingly complex functions, information and levels of identification are stratified) and of an essential *spiritual* principle which renders that and everything else re-conductible to the same origins.

The soul of each thing is a *combination* of information, functions, memories, experiences and meanings to which we give the generic name *'node of complexity'*. Every form, be it an elemental structure, inorganic or a living Form, can be individuated inside a cycle of existence in which *functions* and therefore *complexity* develops. At the end of the cycle, or the given temporal unit, characteristic of that 'Form', the complexity produced – even though it may be only partial in respect to the completeness of consciousness – is little by little transferred into a commensurate 'successive' Form adapted to receive and develop it. Or else the 'Form' will no longer be identifiable as such and transform itself into something successive, different, which in turn will associate itself with a 'successive' level of complexity. Every thing is born, evolves, reproduces and dies. And is then reborn.

Thus we have, on the one hand the evolution of Form as a *supporting structure* obedient to the universal laws and on the other, the evolution of complexity, or significance, that is more or less elementary and of which everything is the bearer. This becomes memory, experience, function and added value: *nodes of complexity* which evolve and when triggered by the divine spark become the *personalities* of the bridge-Form.

In fact, if we consider the bridge-Form as that which is adapted to host the *divine spark*, the nodes of complexity that it

128

contains become the 'personalities' we talked about earlier when looking at the structure of the human soul.

Furthermore, our perception of the personalities does not only focus on their material constitution, nor concentrate on their more subtle aspects such as character, way of being and expression, to represent their higher value. The human species on this planet, in this era, is still a bridge-Form, despite the fact that, as such, it lacks awareness and does not know how to fully express its divine prerogative as a result of a series of historical motives connected to the journey of humans in this world.

The Mapping of the Soul's Personalities

Every individual, in his/her wholeness, expresses their self by means of different principal personalities; each one presents itself to reality as the practical guide of the psycho-physical vehicle, normally following a circadian rhythm or on the basis of precise stimuli.

These personalities – definable as 'expressions of the self', or of the lower self – are not all present contemporaneously in our consciousness, in fact the so-called conscious part (that which makes us say 'ego sum') corresponds to the personality that presents itself on the basis of a certain pattern, that is, to the 'dominant of the moment' which, in its turn is incapable of completely and directly perceiving itself.

We always have a very limited perception, a rather vague and approximate 'average' of what we really are and of the drives that motivate us.

Thus we reduce reality into a principal conventional plane in just the same way that we react to ourselves: we define a presumed identity moment by moment like the prevailing media and its dynamic thrusts,[28] the result of the characters that convulsively emerge and re-emerge from the unconscious, the most conflictual often being among them.

We need to be aware of our many parts, not just to affirm them as such but as a profound 'user' of that, which we really are, a spiritual centre, a soul which uses those self same expressions as instruments, as senses to explore, understand and evolve.

According to the Theory of Personalities, by taking turns or on the basis of acquired rhythms, these personalities dominate the 'individual'. The objective of growth is therefore to really get to know ourselves, to deal with inner conflicts and to integrate and maintain a balance between all our various parts, enhancing their particular talents and giving them a common direction in the interest of the whole (that is ourselves). The first step in order to achieve this is self-observation, without identifying too much with oneself (or with the 'self' of that particular moment) and having individuated when the personalities are close by, learning to recognize them.

The so-called practice of *remembering the self* - of better still of 'being in the present' – is the most useful method for learning to observe ourselves and for beginning to understand internal mechanisms. This moves the barycentre of our identity towards the centre, or the real self (the 'centre of permanent gravity' as the Italian musician Franco Battiato calls it, a clear reminder of the teachings of Gurdjieff).

---

[28] In fact it is impressed upon us by the environment, education, social and moral conventions etc (the
Freudian 'super-I').

Be careful though: our 'expressions' must be recognized and mapped but not nourished in their individualism and separation! Do not insist on the division: they are you! Only and always you! We have to be constantly conscious of our global identity. If you think that the self-analysis is producing a result other than the reassembly of your personalities to benefit your centre - to that which you are as an essence and unique synthesis - then immediately suspend the analysis because this means you are making a mistake in your methods or you have not yet reached the necessary maturity.

Integrating the various parts of yourself into a working system does not only mean resolving your own small or large inner conflicts but specializing your own personalities and knowing how to consciously recognize, manage and call them up. In this way the contrast between the various personalities is no longer a motive for disharmony, or even pathology but rather compensation and equilibrium, exchange and constructive confrontation.

According to studies which range from the psychosomatic to the exploration of our subtle anatomy, every personality presides over precise physical organs and influences their functions. In practice they constitute the subtle and 'auric' structure of the individual. We have to consider that every one of our expressions and masks has its own particular experience, course of formation, memories, way of thinking and integrating with reality as a result of a long history that goes beyond the current incarnation.

Every personality constitutes the experiential content of a series of 'vital cycles' and in its turn, a kind of 'individuality' that, inside the soul system assumes a real function in the expression of talents and specific abilities which, through action should contribute to the growth of the whole. However, each personality also has its own limits, blocks and *karmic* baggage to get rid of and wants to stand out[29]. Only a *happy* interaction – *the result of a more profound awareness* – with other soul personalities allows the personalities to find equilibrium again in an existential expression that is solid and unified.

As we know well, the personalities of an individual are not all 'awake', in fact, the so-called conscious part is governed by an expression that dominates at a given moment and which the person is normally aware of for a very low percentage of time: the rest is 'unconscious'. The unconscious in turn has become a justification for avoiding responsibility for what we are and what we do and for the commitment of *being*.

The personalities work shifts that generally tend to establish themselves into a circadian rhythm and dominate the individual. On the one hand each of them wants to affirm itself, often by prevaricating over the others, on the other they search for integration and a natural balance. This helps to establish a common direction towards the integration of experiences and the re-integration of the divine essence of which deep down they are all the bearer. All of this is done following their own nature.

The cohabitation of these component parts constitutes our whole and represents the vehicle, with all its personalities/ports of our divine exploratory essence, not distinct, but rather fused together with our human aspects which develop little by little.

---

[29] To tell the truth the personalities will naturally tend to integrate but it is the ego that insinuates the idea of conflict and competition, just like the deceptions of the mind which make us insist on defining reality and illusory aspirations.

There are many valid systems for getting to know and therefore 'mapping' one's own soul system: from astrology to the *enneagram*, from the observation of the self to dowsing, from the use of a diary – which can become a real spiritual practice - to the use of dreams, as a neutral environment for a conscious comparison of personalities. The aim is to develop a 'feeling' that goes way beyond the methods and mapping.

There are also many different group practices that can form a valid instrument for analyzing the self through other people: family constellations, systemic analyses and many others. Be careful though - I have to remind you – not to be too taken in by 'mental' schemes and choose wherever possible the more holistic, transpersonal and energetic techniques.

Do not try to understand everything and everyone but let yourself go in a great spirit of silent and attentive self-observation. Allow the selves and the Self to delicately emerge without jumping to conclusions: there is nothing to resolve, just let things 'come out'. It is a meditative act that needs to be guided by the heart rather than the reason, with love rather than science.

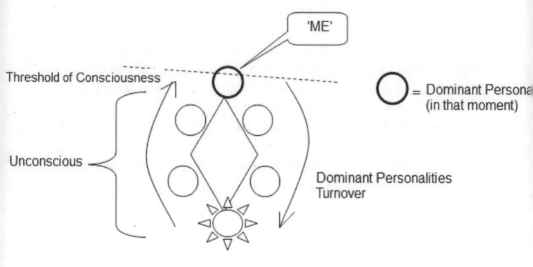

Our Personalities - from Conflict to Harmony

They all call themselves I, that is, they all consider themselves the boss and not one of them wants to acknowledge any other.
G. I. Gurdjieff

On the basis of the frequency and the way in which the different 'expressions of ourselves' alternate in the driving seat, we can sketch out a sort of conventional map of our dominant masks, distinguishing them as:

- *Principal personalities*: which present as the driver according to an established rhythm
- *Secondary personalities*: that present themselves 'in combination' with a principal personality (as

'passengers' in the cockpit, present and receptive but not at the wheel)

- *Marginal personalities*: that show up occasionally in certain situations and under particular stimuli.

Every personality presides over the subtle parts and precise physical organs of the body influencing their functions[30]. Sometimes when competing for dominance a personality entering into conflict with an antagonist, 'attacks' the physical organ to which the latter corresponds. Numerous therapeutic paths exist based upon different methods of intervening in the individual personalities, often integrated with psychotherapeutic approaches and advanced hypnosis techniques . It is important to intervene in the personality in which the origin of a determined problem resides: sometimes we undertake years of psychotherapy that proves inconclusive simply because the work is conducted on a healthy personality rather than calling up and working on the 'sick' one, or on the one that hosts the trauma or the cause of the disturbance.

Now let's look at the following conventional scheme which classifies and takes into consideration the principal dominant personalities that are normally found in an individual soul structure.

---

[30] The opposite is also true!

BASIC MAP REFERENCE OF THE DOMINANT PERSONALITIES

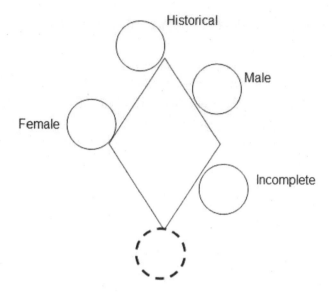

The *historical* personality (the *historical individual* as the Hermeticists called it) is the most 'ancient' component of the group, the one that has stratified the most experiences and through which one can best identify an existential 'conducting thread'.

The *masculine* and *feminine* personalities are those that prevalently express one or the other principle and correspond to different ways of managing our perceptions and the interpretation of reality. The *incomplete* personality, even though found among the dominants, is the youngest and usually the most immature and is therefore easily recognizable.

The personality in formation – sketched out – does not in itself ever dominate, but its presence inside the *cockpit at the side of the dominant of the moment,* is always constant and active in someway. It is one of its prerogatives and triggers a very important mechanism which will be described later.

This simple conventional scheme indicates the basic components of the dominant personalities. With specific hypnosis techniques and thanks to precise methods of observation and self-control, it is possible to become the 'lucid medium of yourself', to thus manage and amplify the expression of the holistic potentiality of your soul, maximising evolutionary processes.

Normally the personalities present themselves casually or according to set rhythms and mechanisms that have been imposed unconsciously by habit. More rarely are they called upon by external stimuli and it is quite difficult to consciously evoke them as if they were instruments.

However, we have to learn (that is teach every one of our personalities) to leave space and to call up the personality – the expression of us – most suited to confront a determined situation or exercise the faculties needed at a particular moment.

It is analogous to times when we instinctively 'prepare ourselves psychologically' to deal with an important or specific event (we call up that part of ourselves which corresponds or which best *responds* to that given performance or necessity).

If we learn to specialize and call up our personalities *ad hoc* we not only learn to progressively identify them with something truer and more profound but we also optimize our learning and performance. We are in fact dominated by our personalities in terms of dominion by the unconscious, by instincts and vague, conflictual and hidden drives – psychology itself could rattle off an infinite number of dynamics in this respect.

It is time to take our lives and ourselves into our own hands. Our thoughts and our emotions, therefore our behaviour and our choices are at the mercy of our dominant of the moment. There are many 'I's and each 'I' wears a different mask and has different desires. We need to learn to observe ourselves and to be responsible and sincere in order to discover our more authentic and profound parts: those parts which can only be liberated by the loving union of soul and reason, masculine and feminine, conscious and unconscious, light and dark.

The Personality in Formation

According to the proposed model, the dominant personality of the moment, the one who is 'at the wheel', is never alone, but carries other personalities with it as if they were 'passengers'. At least one is fixed: *the personality in formation*.

A willingness to listen to the suggestions of passengers depends on the level of integration reached between the various personalities but the dominant personality is always constrained to measure itself against different 'opinions'. We can say that the dominant of the moment is *reason* while the rest are the *soul*: a deeper, closer and truer feeling because they are less involved in external processes and more in contact with the inner self, the profound, the divine essence. Reason explains but the soul feels. Reason calculates but the soul knows and sees further.

However, it is reason that is nearer to evolutionary functions, the probe with which the soul explores and knows. Each one has need of the other. In a harmonious soul structure everything is fluid, the various parts alternate in the roles of reason and soul like an engine. At other times though, let's say in our normal lives, our different parts are in conflict with one another and fight to affirm themselves, one at the expense of another, obscuring our essence.

Going back to the previous example, the presence of 'passengers' in the driver's cockpit and above all the presence of the personality in formation, triggers doubt, that indispensible element in transformation and evolution. What is there to stop a personality from simple re-proposing its 'character' at different times, in other situations and circumstances? Is it sufficient that it changes its space-time context to encourage the evolution of the individual? Are we so willing to change, to overcome our limits and pre-conceptions? Certainly not. The evolutionary process is not determined by just the one personality that is dominant at the time, by whoever is guiding consciousness or at the 'wheel' but includes the contribution of all the other 'passengers', in particular the one that is difficult to manage: the personality in formation.

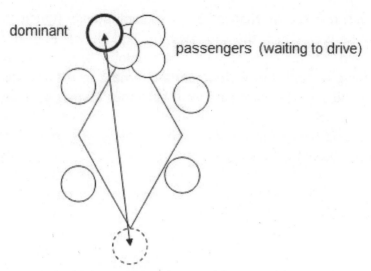

The 'developing personality' interacts and generates DOUBT

The mind tends to be lazy and take the line of least resistance, it loves habit and basically does not favour change, so long as we continue to think in that way. However, we always know what we are doing: there is no unconscious, there is no good faith, there is no ignorance to hold on to.

We can deceive ourselves and do everything we can not to hear the voice of consciousness, nevertheless it exists. But we often prefer not to hear it.

In fact, paradoxically, we fall into self-criticism without acquiring the stimulus for real improvement. Here then is the importance of being kind to oneself, to overcoming the sense of guilt and resistance and of moving towards the growth of our being with great serenity.

The masculine personalities, by nature more *technical* or 'rational' are used in a logical-sequential type of reasoning and take refuge in the proximity of the left hemisphere of the brain: easily using this (male) part which is more in keeping with them. On the contrary the feminine personalities, more suited to the use of creative thought, imagination and intuition, favour the use of the right hemisphere (female), the storehouse of these characteristics.

Here we have to limit ourselves to generally accepted affirmations without setting out the neurophysical details: it is enough to consider that the right and left hemispheres of our brain are mostly in charge of the different functions traditionally associated with masculine and feminine principles: the rational and the intuitive.

The personality in formation will automatically use the complementary hemisphere in respect to that which is used by the dominant personality, with the aim of intensifying the comparison and encouraging the use of more ample logic. Therefore if the dominant is masculine, the personality in formation becomes feminine and stimulates the right part of the brain and vice versa.

In addition, it is thought that only the personality in formation shares our biological age: the others express themselves according to their own maturity which can correspond, using a conventional form of measurement, to different ages in respect to our anagraphic age. This not only results in character disorders but can also have a physical effect, through the organs. A particular organ may correspond to a young personality or an old one and this can reveal itself in different states of functioning and health, over and above the biological rhythm influenced by such configurations (as in the *biological clock* of the body and its specific organs).

Now let's try to metaphorically explain the individual structure as a collective concept: imagine humanity as one great soul, with its personalities (the various human systems, peoples, nations, or more simply each one of us as an individual personality of a cosmic consciousness). Elaborating a little on this hypothesis, it is very interesting to verify once again how the macro and microcosm correspond to one another. As Kahlil Gibran said: "Your neighbour is your unknown self made visible".

Personality and Memory

Every personality has its own sector at its disposition in the memory of the individual, which is deposited entirely in the unconscious, or in the soul structure in its totality and beyond, given that we are the terminals of a much, much vaster 'mental' system[31].

Talking about the unconscious is very reductive and is often used as a justification for trying to avoid responsibility. It might be better to speak of submersed personalities, directions, or of something that we definitely are, or feel we are, and of which we have to resume full control.

Every piece of information, data, idea and experience is recorded by the dominant personality of the moment, according to their own criteria. Every dominant is a kind of archivist who uses its own method of archiving data in its own sector. Access to all the information is always open to all

---

[31] We do not perceive the great vastness and therefore 'outside' of ourselves only because we do not master our real expansion!

personalities regardless of who recorded it in the dominant phase. But as each personality has its own method of archiving, only the dominant personality has direct access to the information that, in its time, it has 'personally' recorded (it archived it so it 'knows' where it is). When it goes to search in someone else's 'circuit' it has to go through all the archive in sequence, to the detriment of reaction time.

Furthermore, a personality receiving its own data has all the information on the *perceptions* and *original sensations* associated with it. A different personality will not be able to track down the original sensations as it can only draw on the basic data which is not interpreted. Therefore, it can only access information concerning the perception which then has to be completed with the sensations/emotions that exist at the moment the search is made or when the information is used.

Generically acquired information certainly exists and all the personalities have direct access to it because it corresponds to the basic programmes necessary for the psycho-physical management of the individual. This means that our basic behaviour, gestures, our way of moving and speaking are not necessarily distinctive elements of one personality rather than another. Instead, the distinctive elements are made up of talents, predispositions and aspects relative to the tastes of the person and the way they react to stimuli, in proportion to their intensity.

Learning happens in a non-consequential manner and is not stratified, given that the personalities alternate according to unconscious mechanisms during the cognitive phase. This can result in gaps or the same information being recorded several times or in memory blanks or difficulty in retrieving information. A lot of information has to be re-inserted so that it can be placed at the disposition of all the principal personalities to guarantee a level of performance that is basically acceptable.

The best results would be obtained if the various personalities consciously accessed the working information used in the management of the individual, to optimize the specialization of each personality in respect to the total synergy. More suitable methods of 'evocation' could be used to substitute the less efficient system of unconscious alternation. Every personality would be eclectic in itself and specialized as regards the whole so that the individual always had the best and the most suitable part of themselves at their disposition in order to live the experiences necessary to evolve.

If the system is coordinated and integrated in the individual, or the individual consciousness, it can avail itself of an optimum psycho-physical vehicle. The method of education and optimization of our various parts does not come together via the mind and mental programmes but rather through the body: it is the body that is the principal system of connection with the memory.

Another aspect to consider is that when we sleep we do not have a dominant: all memory with its direct access is at the disposition of all the personalities, present contemporaneously. When we wake up the personality dominant at the time remembers what we have dreamed. At other times during the day, we may remember different dreams from the night before which correspond to the various personalities as they slowly arrive. When we interpret a dream we need to start from the personality that generated it, highlighting the personality by noting its symbolism, its desires, its repression and its power.

It is interesting to note that during 'the subliminal states' or RITUAL, DREAM and ECSATSY, which are real doors on the infinite, dominant personalities do not exist but the whole of our soul is present, regardless of whether we are aware of it or not, or whether we are able to benefit from such an extraordinary and simultaneously active state of being.

The restriction of consciousness does not allow us to be conscious of it and therefore we never live in a reality that is anything but ordinary.

Occasionally, however, certain sensations, relative to particularly intense events, stray from the dominant of the moment, to leave their 'mark' on other personalities that have been involved in it. This is what happens in the case of trauma.

To cure the consequences of a negative traumatic episode – according to this theory – it would be necessary to recall and act upon the personality that had lived the trauma in order to process and mitigate the negative aspects linked to the original sensations (restructuring), which only that particular personality can recover from its archive.

Obviously the aim would be to direct the cure by going back to the personality that hosts the cause of the disturbance and through it re-establish the necessary equilibrium.

Reincarnation and Reconnection

Everything is exactly
as it should be.
But this, now,
means nothing.

From my Diary -1998

From our point of view, experience in the material world of Form concludes with the physical death of the individual, the soul leaves this world: the attractor 'makes its return' to the Real, while the personalities – more or less reintegrated are left on the other side, on the threshold, where they find a different destiny.

When all the personalities of a soul structure are well integrated – which implies a good relationship between the mind and the heart, perception and feeling, calculating and intuiting – the human experience can express itself in harmony with the evolutionary aims of the divine spark, reach *enlightenment* or become conscious of itself as a fragment of the divine in evolution.

This is awareness of the self, harmony and reconciliation; it breaks the link with conditioned reason and the ego. It is the goal of spirituality.

Having arrived at this state of consciousness guided by the divine identity, the personalities/souls can grow until they complete their experience in the material world in the evolutionary process of consciousness. We can imagine that once they have completed their experience, they 'fuse' with the attractor and on the death of the physical body, but not necessarily, *attain the Real*, reuniting with the primeval divinity, carrying with them the results of their experience (added value).

If the opposite is the case, if they do not achieve completion, they have to remain in transit on the Threshold[32] until such

----

[32] The *Threshold* – according to the jargon typical of esoteric physics – is an intermediary state of being between Form and the Real. It is an inter-realm between parallel worlds containing the routes and super-symmetries which

time as they are re-projected into the material world of Form to achieve the requisite result (reincarnation).

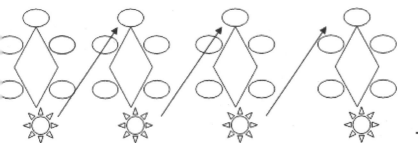

We need to look into the process that leads to ultimate realization in more depth, it is certainly not as linear as one would want it to be but it can, nevertheless, be achieved during the course of our life.

We have to remember that our integrity, which is dependent upon the divine barycentre, always has to provide the background: we are a totality and we have to insist upon our unity and not on separation. However, it is didactically useful to use the image composed and expressed by our soul in order to understand particular mechanisms and to recognize that our sense of separation is illusory and misleading.

---

facilitate travel from one system of laws to another. The Threshold is the 'environment' in which complexity sustains itself without the direct need for a material support.

In practice the Threshold contains 'quantities' – still incomplete – of organized complexity that, in order to evolve and complete themselves live in symbiosis with Form while remaining substantially outside of it (entity or divinity), or cyclically re-entering Form (as souls) through the mechanism of reincarnation.

We know that the personalities are *individualities* in their own right. We could think of them as 'shopping bags' that our divine consciousness slowly fills with experiences in the supermarket of life. Let's imagine that we are out *shopping* but the bag keeps breaking and we keep losing things. We no longer know which things are ours or what belongs to other people and we are completely lost in the supermarket!

Every personality, has its own experience, formation, memories, way of thinking and interacting with reality. From incarnation to incarnation – if we want to use this commonly adopted logical sequence – we always consist of a new combination of personalities. Among them we will more or less find, in proportion to the level of integration effectively attained, a shared evolutionary line which is coherent and continuous; one that is able to establish a precise conducting thread consisting of the same evolving consciousness from one existence to another.

The continuous line of an individual is potentially represented by the personality in formation which becomes the dominant in the successive soul structure.

In fact, this personality, beginning 70/90 days from the birth of the physical body, progressively forms during the life span of the individual and finally gathers inside itself the experiential synthesis of the personalities that make up the soul structure. It thus contains the entire evolutionary significance of that incarnation in a distilled form.

Ideally the integrated personalities unite and fuse together in the personality in formation, which – if its evolutionary mission is not concluded in a single life span, as is quite probable, presents as the historical personality in the successive structure. It continues on until it contains all the experience necessary to complete its evolutionary mission and fuse with the divine spark in the Absolute (we can imagine it fusing with the attractor itself).

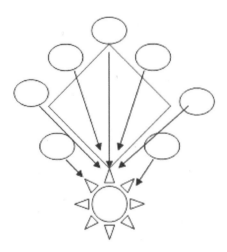

The first step towards spiritual growth therefore, is to realize that there is a unity of intent among your own recognized and integrated personalities. They are like parts of a whole which, depending on what we are complessively at the end of the life-cycle, fuse into the personality in formation. This latter could present itself, together with other personalities, which in their turn are attracted to that particular structure (according to the evolutionary criteria of compatibility previously discussed), in the system of a successive soul: that is, in the following incarnation as a formed personality and bearer of complexity in evolution (historical dominant).

And so it goes on: another personality will form and acquire, successively, together with others, the result of this new incarnation until enough experiences have been gathered to complete Consciousness which, at least in theory, a bridge-Form should have the power to achieve in just one incarnation. However, it normally does not happen that way.

We are not only slow in achieving the project of consciousness in a single incarnation, thus in fully expressing the absolute intelligence potential that we have but that same incarnation can result in a completely incoherent process, that is at times totally ineffectual! Given the current conditions of humans on the planet, it would seem that a complex course of 'reawakening' is necessary in order to develop the evolutionary process.

We have to remember that even though we are using these examples from the soul's point of view, time does not actually exist: we are talking about an activation of states in the simultaneousness of a multi-dimensional existence.

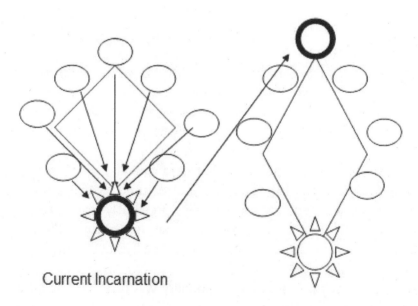

Current Incarnation

Next Incarnation

The determination of the 'successive' evolutionary context is a natural process in which each person is basically the only and ultimate judge of themselves. However, various esoteric traditions relate, superior spiritual processes that could involve divine forces or disincarnate entities appointed to judge the individual (for example in Theosophical tradition they are called the 'Lords of Karma') and, as universal principles of reference exist, we can imagine such forces as the entities in charge of those principles.

The resulting incarnation for each personality – including that recently formed which has incorporated the others into itself (remember, this only happens if the personalities are sufficiently integrated with one another) - has to position itself in the space-time that promises the most suitable evolutionary opportunities, which can be in the chronological future or past in respect to the previous incarnation. By the way, the 'weighing' of the soul happens outside of time and not being subject to any sequential chronological constraints, allows for an evaluation on a strictly evolutionary level, one that certainly does not include our common idea of progress.

Searching for a Way Out: Who Am I?

So-called 'past lives research' is the fruit of a very limited vision of the totality of our identity and evolutionary processes. Past lives do not exist. We are a multi-dimensional presence in time which is contemporaneous and simultaneous in respect to the scanning (from the past to the future) which is produced by our present mind.

Research into *past lives* can be an incentive: a past life is nothing more than a *representation* of us, that can perhaps play an instrumental role on a psycho-therapeutic level. It can be used as a method but we are not talking about something real

151

in itself, at least not in the way it is habitually described and advertised.

We can easily imagine in such an environment the incongruity of proposing the possibility of *programming reincarnations*. Primarily because a future incarnation is certainly not our aim. Furthermore it is not possible to interfere with the processes of nature, at least only if you are talking about manipulating the not yet inviolable individual essence, in as much as those parts which are not integrated with that essence can in someway be the seat of memories, and produce physical and vital energy that is useful for the maintenance of egregors (εγρεγοριεν) and their relative parasitic systems (religions, cults, and so on).

Obviously to manipulate the non-integrated parts and put them back into constant circulation inside a given energetic circuit, the integration of the personalities and the free evolution of consciousness is not to be encouraged; the continuous recycling of incomplete, non-directed energies and succubae personalities is created instead.

Returning to past lives research, we also need to consider the complex mechanism of the personalities and their dispersion from life to life which makes it extremely difficult to trace the course of their temporal path in the various soul systems.

Since each one of us is multi-dimensional totality simultaneously immersed in the folds of time, we can only talk about the search for the self: not of past or future or parallel lives, or whatever, only of a search for the 'Self' or the totality of our lives in all their extensions:

- Our current life, as the search for our inner selves
- Our life beyond contemporaneity, as the search for our authentic extensions of consciousness.

152

This is why instead of searching for the re-composition of the self through a knowledge of past lives, following the classic logic of reincarnations, we should be talking about reconnection: seizing hold of the contemporaneous and simultaneous consciousness of our own real identity: the individuation and connection of our own parts, rediscovered and recognized throughout time, space and the dimensions, be they real or potential, so that they can in turn integrate into a higher evolutionary scenario.

It is from the current reawakening, in fact, by correspondence that we determine the design of our soul in time and therefore reconnect our various parts. In practice we *set up* past lives rather than find them, entering into resonance with parts of our Consciousness that are evolving through time.

Activating the reconnection with our better, more harmonious and healthier parts, be it on the psycho-physical plane or that of the spiritual, means recalling events and states and also resolving the problems that relate to them. The process described could work by applying the therapeutic concept of reconnection that is presently in vogue. However, that dynamic, which is secondary in respect to a holistic reconnection, if extrapolated and solicited outside of an organic pathway or applied with superficiality (at times characterized by certain current New Age directions), could reveal itself to be misleading or even counterproductive.

We have seen that, from incarnation to incarnation, we are made up of a combination of personalities that is always different and which may or may not find a shared and continuous evolutionary line on the basis of their level of synergic integration. The continuous line of an individual should ideally be represented by the personality in formation which, a short while after physical birth, arrives to support those selected by the attractor and in turn evolves during the life of the person. This 'new' personality specifically identifies the current incarnation and if the structure is sufficiently harmonious, will synthesize into itself all the other personalities, to present itself – if necessary – in the soul system of the *successive* incarnation as the 'historical personality' together with other personalities that have been selected.

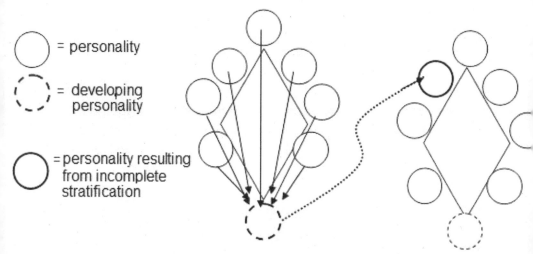

= personality

= developing personality

= personality resulting from incomplete stratification

The same discourse applies to the latter: they can be personalities that derive from a stratification (complete or partial) – or from a dispersion - that the attractor has assembled in the new structure according to the criteria we have already discussed.

A disharmonious life that is privy of meaningful experiential content in order to achieve a real and complete evolution, creates a 'short circuit' that impedes the personality in formation from recognizing and representing the others. In the successive incarnation the personalities that are not harmonized are dispersed into other structures. In practice, evolution attempts to keep going until a reawakening of consciousness is achieved and a 'way out is found'.

The continued disassembling of the soul from one life to another, is what normally happens to the terrestrial human being over a long period of time and for many different reasons. It is a phenomenon that impedes growth and the stratification of experiences and, consequently, the completion of the personality and consciousness.

The unified and defined 'self' does not exist, therefore: there are only 'selves' and each one of them, even though competing with the constitution of a certain instantaneous 'self', is not the 'self'.

Maurice Percheron - Buddha

The personalities once loose in the beyond, are not only dispersed for the previously described motives but are often destined to continuous impoverishment, controlled and engulfed by egregors, predatory forces and entities of various levels that participate in a spiritual and divine eco-system which is no longer in harmony with evolution. They are the expressions of 95% of those mysterious 'shadowy' realities and, or ourselves, that stop us from living in harmony with every manifestation of being and inner life that is part of the vital eco-system of this universe.

In a situation of this kind, the only possibility we have of identifying ourselves with a continuous individual principle is to find our identity again and place it in the *inner divine principle*.

Only by doing this can we reach an absolute spiritual barycentre that connects to our *being* dispersed in time and establishes continuity in our identity. We can then express a sense that unites the past, present and future[33] and understand our Spiritual Mission (*Chiah*)[34].

The man with the divided, complicated, contradictory soul is not helpless: the core of his soul, the divine force in its depths, is capable of acting upon it, changing it, binding the conflicting forces together, amalgamating the diverging elements – is capable of unifying it. This unification must be accomplished before a man undertakes some unusual work.

Martin Buber –
The Way of Man According to the Teachings of Hasidism

From another point of view we could say that the personalities which incarnate – and of which we find ourselves composed – are nothing more than incomplete parts: waste products of existential process that have to be put back into circulation to reach their evolutionary potential and completion. It is not the spiritual soul that transmigrates to perfect itself (as in Hinduism) but rather the uncompensated *karma*, the ego that is not disposed of, or if we prefer, the parts that are still weighed down by our personal baggage which do not relate to the same spiritual essence and still have to be put to the test in order to exalt and purify the self.

---

[33] Let's keep in mind that on a spiritual plane everything happens contemporaneously: time is a 'territory'.

[34] This life could be the 'fulcrum' in determining who we are, who we were, and who we will be: it depends on our willingness to search and grow authentically.

This perspective could conciliate the concept of monotheisms, which tend to avoid the issue of reincarnation[35], with the processes described up to now in which the structures of the soul are protagonists in the dimensions of time. For example, Buddha considered the 'I' as a mere mnemonic abstraction composed of recorded memories – which gives a false impression of continuity. The only valid Self is that of the given moment: one must therefore concentrate on immediate experience. Painful dualism makes its appearance the moment in which the individual tries to make the practically inexistent 'I' act.

If the various personalities constituting the individual integrate in a balanced and functioning equilibrium, thus acquiring a common evolutionary direction, when physical death intervenes they remain connected to one another (amalgamated in the personality formed during life) and re-propose themselves for inclusion in the 'successive' soul structure, little by little stratifying experiences, memories and values.

---

[35] Whether it be mono or polytheistic, the concept of reincarnation is to be found in every religion in which an absolute energy presides over creation and the destruction of the world, in a cyclical process of birth and death which is continuously renewed.

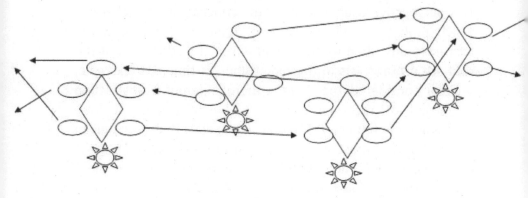

Dispersion of Personalities

However some of them disperse and their destinies separate into different *attractors*. That is caused by the splitting off of individual personalities that do not manage to reach, in the course of vital dynamics, that syntony that is potentially the basis for the criteria that define the composition of the soul structure.

Consequently, spiritual harmony which is ideally created from the compatibility of the personalities and their ability to share growth in a given context, is then demonstrated through *free will* and growth seen as conquest.

The dispersion of certain personalities makes reassembling a coherent picture of the human soul somewhat problematic and makes 'past lives research' rather meaningless.

Who are we in this moment? And who were we if our preceding constituent parts were scattered time after time into perpetually differing and incoherent structures? The various personalities construct themselves in unendingly different interlacings and successively transit new individualities.

It is important to remember that to conduct a coherent inner search you need to individuate the spiritual barycentre of your current life and consequently recompose your own experiential design (be it extended in the past or the future given that the evolutionary sequence is not subject to chronological evaluation) not in an arbitrary way but consistent with the quality of your own divine identity.

The reawakening is a non-local phenomenon which produces its effects simultaneously – like a spiritual *entanglement* – on all of our recomposed temporal body, depending upon and in resonance with the reawakening of our consciousness.

The reiterated dispersion, has become a dynamic to which our way of being has become accustomed, so much so, that it considers the inner disharmony which is the source of our cyclical spiritual dispersion in time as *normal*. Dispersion, that during our life can cause serious inner conflict and even result in psychological disturbance or disease in the body.

The individual who intends to integrate all the different parts of his/herself and acquire control of them, explore the inner self through them and recall them to enforce a common evolutionary direction, has to learn to 'love' his/herself. It may seem rhetorical, but *love* is the key to deeply accepting, welcoming and understanding the self. It is also the key to understanding what you really want from life, so that you can find happiness and fulfil your role in the world. That act of love is not egoistically self-referential but means being in tune with yourself and your own evolutionary mission. Lived experience assumes a non-casual logic when it relates to a search which aims at reaching profound harmony.

Love, meant as acceptance and communion, is the access key, the cement, between the various personalities. Each one of us has to 'fall in love with him/herself', or better still has to make their personalities fall in love with one another.

We are using the term 'fall in love' to underline the emotional aspect of this inner process of union, in the sense of being purified of egoistical or narcissistic implications arriving from an invasive dominant. Today, in effect, we are dominated by our personalities and our body; our thoughts and emotions are at the mercy of the dominant of the moment; just as if we were sleepwalkers. To draw closer to Consciousness, it is necessary to re-appropriate the completeness of ourselves and rediscover our essential and authentic centre. Our personalities can only fuse with the divine cup or our inner Grail, thanks to the warmth of love. This is called 'The Alchemical Work'.

Knowing your own personalities and defining their talents and experiences ensures that they relate to one another in common fellowship, overcome conflicts and indentify themselves as part of a more complex structure. It is the necessary path towards becoming *aware*.

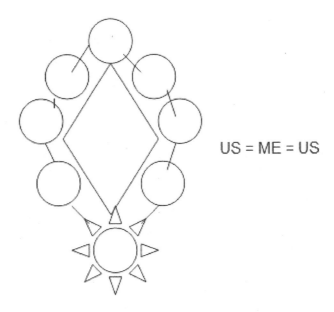

US = ME = US

It is a process that begins with self-observation and proceeds by applying precise techniques. The preciousness of and the need to compare yourself with the external environment, the events of life and with people close to you in order to achieve a solid and recognizable pathway of change, is evident. It manifests through our explicit relationship with reality, over and above our personal convictions, and yet it is always centred on the self and its own true will.

The personalities with more logical temperaments which are inclined towards mental processes that are logical-sequential mostly use the left-side of the brain. Those personalities more suited to creative thought which use the imagination and intuition mostly use the right-side of the brain. This means that the integration of the personalities requires an integration of the different kinds of logic employed in interpreting reality

161

which, in alchemical allegory, corresponds to the inner masculine and feminine principles being reunited.

The perfect integration of the personalities implies – on an alchemical level – the reintegration of the Androgen, or the integration of the two poles through which we express our vital energies and perceive and interpret events. The integration is therefore a fundamental step on the road to enlightenment and Consciousness. Without it we cannot fully comprehend reality, meet and know ourselves, intuit the power of magic thought, live in communion with reality, defeat ignorance and fear, intervene in material phenomena, or emancipate ourselves from all restriction and attain the Real.

Man is a divided being, contradictory, complicated, but he can know the miracle of unification by putting his own will in synergy with the divine force that lies in his depths.

Enzo Bianchi, Prior of the Monastic Community of Bose (Italy)

In extreme synthesis our current scenario opens up two possibilities:

1. If during the course of life the various constituent personalities of the individual integrate in a balanced functioning relationship and acquire a common evolutionary direction, at physical death, having been left on the *threshold*, they remain linked together and tend to re-propose themselves to the attractor of the successive incarnation. They coagulate into one personality and together with others make up a new soul structure. Every soul structure will contain

numerous syntheses of lived experiences (in different times and on different planes), until it arrives at a structure with information that is complete or significant enough to exit from the *cycle of incarnations.*

2. If there is no awareness and harmony between the soul's personalities from one life to another they will disperse and their destinies will be separated among different attractors, making it very difficult to pick out a line of consistent *individual continuity* from the various incarnations.

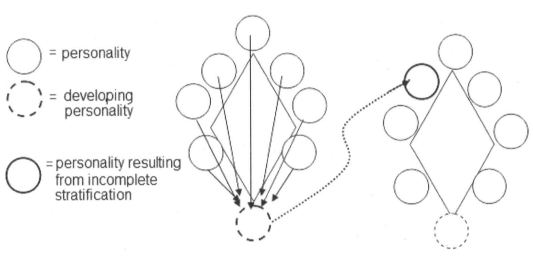

◯ = personality

◌ = developing personality

◯ = personality resulting from incomplete stratification

Ok then, but, who is the real 'me'?

I am not just the personality of the moment or the sum of the personalities of my current soul structure or the structures scattered throughout time, and not even the divine spark of this or other specific personalities. **I can only be the divine essence that I am able to reawaken in this present life, in that**

it is a true and radical spiritual identity; the centre of the soul system that constitutes me. And, consequently with this understanding my 'body of consciousness' – by correspondence - in all its simultaneous and contemporary incarnations will go and determine itself.

The Race to the 'Real'

According to Tradition each one of us is entrusted with a 'Higher Self', a *God* (or fragment of God) which, by living the experiences of our lower self, can evolve. If the evolution of consciousness and the completion of our 'Mission' happens during the life of our physical vehicle (the body) or coincides with the cycle of our biological life, we are then faced with an ideal process in which we as bridge-Form support our vital and spiritual nature. If this is not the case it means that our spiritual identity, which is incomplete in regard to evolutionary potential, has to complete itself in someway. According to certain schools and religions this can mean, completing life and human experience by reincarnating. To others, it means perfecting on the other side or both, following the theory in which one part has to reincarnate while the other more evolved part remains on higher levels of reality.

On the basis of the level achieved, the identity that reincarnates may be aware of its own 'conducting thread' or may lose its memory, just as the spiritual part will have a greater or lesser awareness of its self. Therefore the being as a whole may or may not be integral and may or may not be aware of its real identity and potential.

To this we have to add that, as far as the soul is concerned, time has no valence: which means it has to realize itself and re-position itself in the best evolutionary context possible be it in the chronological past or in the future in respect to the individuation of a particular incarnation.

Just as divine consciousness intends to learn, grow, reassemble and rediscover itself through the experience of this relative reality to finally reunite with the All from which it 'comes', in the same way the lower self can increase its own level of awareness in order to identify with something more expansive and transcendent. A meeting has to take place in our inner selves, a recognition of intent and nature, 'as Above so Below': such is the nature of the *Alchemical Marriage*, a new 'anomalous wave', a new meeting of forces and different natures from which other expressions of consciousness and new universes are born!

The divine spark is the bearer of extraordinary senses and faculties which can be used to awaken ourselves but its most significant and relevant attribute is its power of *free will*, through which we can extricate ourselves from the labyrinth of multiplicity and choices and turn a mere mechanical process of existence into one that is evolutionary and aware.

Enlightenment

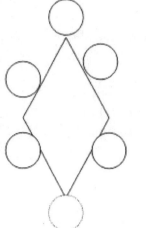
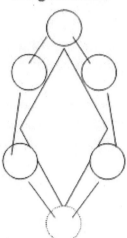

Metamorphosis

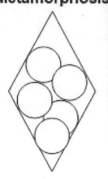

When a soul has completely and totally exhausted its experience, it fuses with the attractor and attains the Real, bringing back to divine Consciousness the wealth that it has developed during its various life cycles.

Ideally, this is achieved in a single life cycle but if not, the soul has to then reach the following stages from cycle to cycle: knowledge of the self, integration (enlightenment) and communion (metamorphosis).

The nature of evolutionary transfiguration is not *also* but *above all* physical. It is a complex spiritual process, basically psycho-alchemical which interfaces with the hyper-dimensions of the continuum through the genetics of our bodily vehicle, transubstantiating it to higher levels of existence. We can only imagine its nature now thanks to fleeting revelations conceded during altered states (or perhaps normalized) of our mind.

166

With the following illustration we can visualize the realization process by looking at it again from different perspectives.

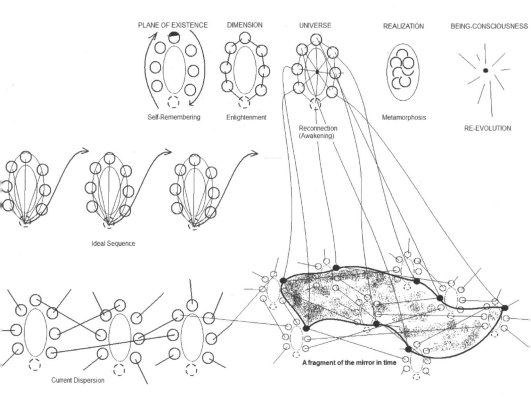

The reconnection of our parts is either the result of a true 'search', that fills the cup of existence to the brim, or else the result of the void that makes room inside of us and, as it were, swallows up those same parts because of the difference in pressure. It is the mystery of the Grail: the always full, the always empty. It is the mystery of the Tao.

The supreme realization, the 'Great Work', or Metamorphosis, is really understood as the transfiguration and transubstantiation of Form, of the body and the mind. It lies in the absolute definitive and eternal incorruptibility of every manifestation, expression and emotion on whatever plane, in its maximum freedom to manifest or not.

Every solution of continuity between Form-threshold-Real vanishes in the absolute freedom of movement and state.

Also the experience of precariousness and death has to be lived in order to rise again and stabilize itself at its best in an ideal manifestation in the totality of being. It is the definitive stabilization of every expression of the Self in its free and everlasting perfection.

The myth of the Christ is perhaps the most complete expression of these terms.

Death and the 'Intelligent Spirit'

From the different traditions and numerous studies on death, be they religious, esoteric or spiritualistic, a rather complex picture emerges of testimonies, experiences and interpretations relative to the phenomena of death, after-death and the possible interaction between the world of the living and that of the dead (in its most diverse meanings and manifestations: from the lowest and most disturbing, to the sublime, bearer of hope and love). It is the true mystery of the real identity of the *being* with which in many different ways and for many different reasons we enter into contact.

And every experience, every message, every interpretation, even though conditioned by beliefs religious convictions or emotion, inevitably leads us to draw different conclusions on life, the soul, history, the other side, reincarnation, 'liberation' and 'salvation'. However, all things considered we can actually arrive at models and scenarios that are coherent even though on the surface they may appear to contradict one another.

We must not be categorical about the fact that contact with the dead has to exclusively favour mere psychological interpretations and necessities or that such phenomena can only be considered possible inside a human context and very specific rituals (the cult of the ancestors, peoples integrated with nature and tribal traditions), or that it simply relates to the interference of parasitic entities (which is often the case).

It is right to consider the phenomenon of 'invisible helpers', of Theosophical memory, placed in the category of angels, or else associate it with the intervention of our dearest, an eventuality that is also supported in religious settings.

In addition we should also consider the so called 'knowledge of and conversations with our own guardian angel' which apart from the catholic acceptance of the term, in esoteric fields - above all *thelemic* - is considered as the possibility of entering into contact with the most evolved part of the self, with one's own *demon,* inner genius or higher Self; an indication that one is becoming aware of one's own divine nature (the 'occult' god).

All these phenomena and their interpretations do not exclude one another: the inspirations and teachings are all valid when we consider their particular standpoint because they support different motivations, priorities and perspectives. The suggestion, deception and self-deception of the mind also plays its part and has a certain psycho-therapeutic function, if not 'pedagogical' and spiritual: certainly we have to exclude bad faith and psychological disturbances from such considerations but we also have to bear in mind that there is a thin line between genius and madness.

Mediumistic contact is possible with the dead, although it is necessary to distinguish between the identity one contacts before the definitive separation of the individual from the material plane (approximately the first 70 days after death) and that of the entity – the expression of the dead person – with whom you wish to relate to after that period.

We can suppose that after our physical death various phases follow and that different parts of us can distinguish themselves, which likewise follow different paths.

There are two fundamental parts to consider:

- One: our identity which represents the best of what we have been and which, if necessary, 'reincarnates'[36] carrying with it the potential conducting thread of our growing experience.
- Two: our 'higher' identity, truer, more authentic and essential that, at different levels in the Beyond, remains and represents us in higher dimensions.

This means that:

- In spite of the subtle waste, resulting from the attachments and obsessions, that can remain on the

---

[36] For reasons of fluidity I will continue to use the idea of reincarnation because I consider valid all that was said before with regard to it but let's not forget the non-locality of evolution in time.

material plane (which generate thought-forms, shells, larvae etc...)

- In spite of the non-integrated personalities that are dispersed
- In spite of that which has been conserved of the personality in formation in the guise of the *successive historical dominant*[37]...

... a spiritual agglomeration can form – more or less intense – from the most integrated and most evolved or highest essence of the person; that part, which in virtue of a certain level of integration, has in some way already penetrated the *attractor*. It is becoming that aspect of personal identity which does not need to reincarnate but can represent, through that specific identity, a testimony, a 'pillar of the bridge' beyond the material world of Form: a reference to the divine and the Real to which it aspires.

It is the conducting spiritual thread, the helper who assists its dearest but above all the Guardian Angel of the 'successive' personal structures which are still incarnate: the higher part of the self that from the Beyond can inspire us and to which we can connect in order to understand the direction of our own evolution.

It is the transcendent reflection of the higher self: the 'Intelligent Spirit', which perhaps Rol referred to or that which, according to the descriptions of certain mediums, accompanies

---

[37] This is the part that is of necessity vampirized by 'out of control' divinities, egregors, paradises, citadels or entities that attempt to subjugate it into a circuit of programmed reincarnations – though in the major part of cases these forces manage to intercept the waste of the least integrated parts, while the more integrated, because of the level they have attained, cannot be so easily subtracted from the natural processes of evolution.

each one of us (often described as a relative – and could in effect also be the *intelligent spirit* of that relative – or else like an 'angel'). Interestingly, for shamans it is the 'allied spirit', which is synonymous with 'ancestor'.

Here we are considering a *continuum* of the soul, not only between different natural or alien dimensions, but *also* – and probably *simultaneously* – ultra-temporal and spiritual in an absolute sense.

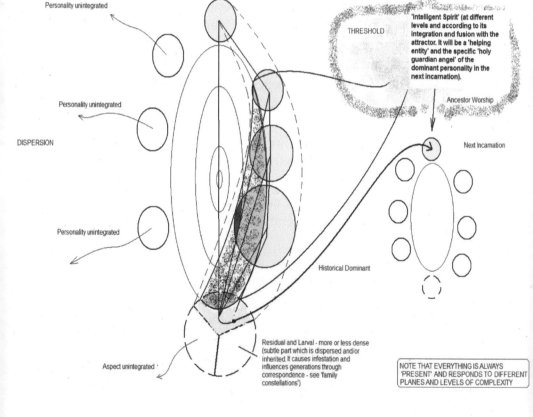

Personality unintegrated

Personality unintegrated

DISPERSION

Personality unintegrated

THRESHOLD

'Intelligent Spirit' (at different levels and according to its integration and fusion with the attractor. It will be a 'helping entity' and the specific 'holy guardian angel' of the dominant personality in the next incarnation).

Ancestor Worship

Next Incarnation

Historical Dominant

Residual and Larval - more or less dense (subtle part which is dispersed and/or inherited. It causes infestation and influences generations through correspondence - see 'family constellations')

Aspect unintegrated

NOTE THAT EVERYTHING IS ALWAYS 'PRESENT' AND RESPONDS TO DIFFERENT PLANES AND LEVELS OF COMPLEXITY

If I enter into contact with an individual the first seventy days after their physical death it is most probable that I will enter into relation with the more human aspects of the person, or else with their 'lower' parts. After seventy days however, it is possible, although not that simple and automatic, to interact with the 'intelligent spirit' (or, it is more likely that the intelligent spirit, if evolved enough, or if need be, will interact with me).

The lowest of the subtle waste, just as potentially the higher aspects – but the first case is more probable – influences or conditions relatives and perhaps friends, from the closest to the more distant, almost like transferred karma or, in other cases, as a very positive quality or faculty, that is transferred by 'correspondence'.

The illustration above provides a synthesis of this model which, though obviously conventional and generalized, takes into account the theories expressed so far.

It is an open field and research quietly continues.

The Power of the Divine Self

Now it should be easier to understand how *Thought* acts on reality and the material world, through correspondence with that which animates everything: the 'intelligent spirit'.

Such interaction does not correspond to our common thought processes, which are fed by illusory perceptions but to the use of Thought on the part of the awakened Self, which is able to perceive beyond the *veil of Maya* and to act on reality in virtue of its re-found consciousness, its unity and communion with all things.

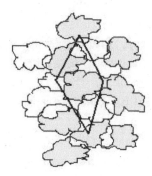

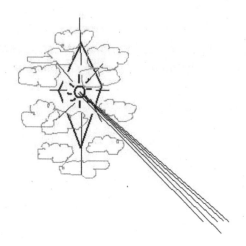

The Higher Self is obscured by the clouds-personalities full off rain-ego-mind.

Only our inner Sun can warm us (love) and allow the rain to fall in a great purifying storm.

Therefore the clouds are lighter and evaporate and allow the sun to shine again (the divine self) from our inner sky (attractor) emanating rays of vital healing energy (power)

Action through one's own spirit on the spirit of all things. The power that is based on the correspondence between our attractor and micro-attractors which subtend the composition of every particle of matter, as described in the illustration, is a power which can be exercised on reality from *outside the laws* that constitute it, by virtue of an upstream force.

Such possibilities – which form part of the essential concept of Magic – exist only on the condition that there is:

1. Perfect integration between the soul personalities
2. Union between heart and mind
3. Awareness of Self and purity of intent.

If only one of these aspects is missing we fall back into exercising a 'power of Maya', or power inside the illusion, exercised through the internal processes of the system: to be precise we are not talking about real power.

By 'real' we mean that power that is capable of sublimating the experience accumulated by the evolutionary life of a unitary consciousness: in the absence of such sublimation any kind of power is but an illusion, a game of mirrors, incompleteness and conflict.
The integration of the personalities is that perfect alignment which allows the inner light to shine through.

This is the power over manifestation and synchronicity, that is able to activate, or better still, at an even higher level of interpretation, 'leave' reality to juxtapose itself to our spiritual will/necessity.

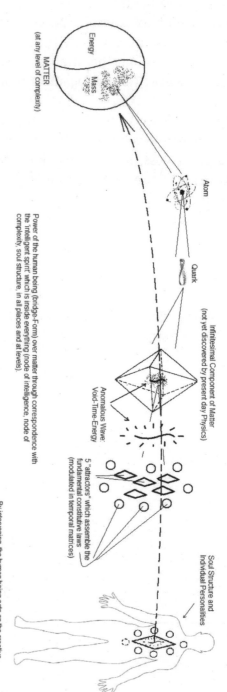

MATTER
(at any level of complexity)

Energy

Mass

Atom

Quark

Infinitesimal Component of Matter
(not yet discovered by present day Physics)

Anomalous Wave:
Void-Time-Energy

5 "attractors" which assemble the
fundamental constitutive laws
(modulated in temporal matrices)

Soul Structure and
Individual Personalities

Power of the human being (bridge-Form) over matter through correspondence with
the 'intelligent spirit' which is inside everything (node of intelligence, node of
complexity, soul structure, in all places and at levels).

By intervening, the human being acts on the creative
composition of matter at all levels and can even add
further programmes and functions (think for example of
the impregnation of objects as in a blessing and to the
consecration of magic instruments). They act as
additional laws in terms of information which is then
managed by the immanent attractors.

176

Reincarnation does not Exist: Another Way of Thinking

Our current life is not real but a convention: an 'average' configured in deference to the mind. Just as the ego, or our vague idea of 'I' , our plane *of existence* results from an average of the whole of reality in which we participate. We do not perceive in its entirety because we are fluctuating chaotically inside it. We limit our perception of reality to just the 'principal' plane of historical existence, which in fact does not exist, in as much as it is only a convention made dense by our individual and collective minds. In the same way, our 'present' life is nothing more than an *averaged out perception* resulting from our multi-dimensional and multi-temporal existence of which we have lost the order and awareness.

Certainly everything depends on this present life: others do not exist!
Nothing else exists. We are not 'somewhere else' in respect to the fictitious perception of our whole existence. If we take to extremes the maya/ matrix theories in which our perception of reality and life is all illusory, then we are not just one frame of a film but all the frames seen from above! Ours is not a life but an approximate and chaotic perception of all that we are contemporaneously. This has more meaning if we accept that true life is of a different nature than the dream we live as real, just as all traditions and Masters have insisted.

Perhaps every level of existence is nothing more than a fantastic stage wound in and around itself. This means that nothing exists except us: not aliens or extra-terrestrials. The same applies to the concept of space with its stars and galaxies, which is nothing more than a magnificent stage set, all set up for us, and we are at the centre of it, on all the levels and possible dimensions that we find ourselves, whether we realize it or not.

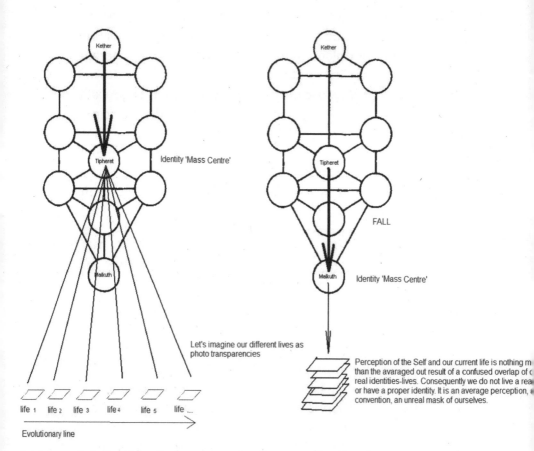

Identity 'Mass Centre'

FALL

Identity 'Mass Centre'

Let's imagine our different lives as photo transparencies

life 1   life 2   life 3   life 4   life 5   life ....

Evolutionary line

Perception of the Self and our current life is nothing m than the avaraged out result of a confused overlap of c real identities-lives. Consequently we do not live a rea or have a proper identity. It is an average perception, e convention, an unreal mask of ourselves.

Our personalities can be likened to the various lives we have experienced throughout our different incarnations.

First of all we have to re-integrate our identity in Tipheret and then become aware of our real Self ('centre of mass' of our consciousness) and of our lives. We need to achieve a unified perception of what-we-are, that is not fragmented into different personalities and illusory states of mind.

This means putting our perception of ourselves and our different parts in time into order. We will then be able to distill the evolutionary meaning of our real life experience (added value) and project it into Kether as the synthesis of our explorations.

178

Thoughts on Magic

Magick takes every thought and act for its apparatus; it has the Universe for its Library and its Laboratory; all Nature is its Subject. [...] There are a great many people who quite misunderstand the nature of Magick. They have an idea that it is something vague and unreal, instead of being, as it is, a direct means of coming into contact with reality.

Aleister Crowley - Magick in Theory and Practice

A universal science exists through which we can know and work on different planes of reality and different levels of Consciousness. Through it we can contact and connect together laws, entities, natural and spiritual forces of whatever order or grade, both inside and outside of us.

Today we might define it as the ' dynamic of the dimensions', or the *science of correspondence* that – calling upon *Hermetic principles*[38]:

---

[38] Hermes Trismegistus is a legendary figure from the Hellenic Age, venerated as a Master of wisdom and the author of the *'Corpus Hermeticum'*. The foundation of the philosophy known as Hermeticism is attributed to him. Hermes Trismegistus literally means 'Hermes the threefold greatest'. With this name he wanted to assimilate Ermete, Greek god of logos, Thoth, the Egyptian god of writing, numbers and geometry. According to the scholar Athanasius Kircher of the XVII century: 'The Arabs called him Idris, the Hebrews Hadores(...), the Phoenicians (...) Tauto, the Egyptians (...) Thot, but also Ptha, and the Greeks Ermete Trismegisto.' Hermeticism had a notable influence over Medieval and Renaissance culture.

- through true Will
- applying the correct Knowledge
- employing the necessary energy

allows us to overcome the limits of space and time, acting *'as Above so Below'*, on *'similar responds to similar'* and where *'Thought creates'*.

During the Renaissance, Magic was correctly referred to as the "Art of making things happen". In fact in its most abstract sense magic was seen as a method of obtaining precise advantages from the relationship between Will, Knowledge and Energy.

More recently, in a certain sense, magic has also been defined as the unknown or forgotten 'science'.

We can read in the *Lemegeton*, or *The Lesser Key of Solomon*, that "Magic is nothing more than the highest, most absolute, divine knowledge of Natural Philosophy, made to progress towards the complete efficacy of its wondrous workings through a correct understanding of the inner and hidden virtues of things…".

Papus (Gérard Encausse, 1865-1916), in his *Methodical Treatise of Practical Magic* says: "Magic is the projection of vital energy driven by the human Will".

Aleister Crowley writes, in his *Magick*:

Magick is the Science and Art of causing change to occur in conformity with Will.
[…]

Man is capable of being and using anything which he perceives, for everything that he perceives is in a certain sense a part of his being. He may thus subjugate the whole Universe of which he is conscious to his individual Will.

[...]

Magick is the Science of understanding oneself and one's conditions. It is the Art of applying that understanding in action.

Effectively in the sixteenth century Jacob Boehme (1575-1624), in his *De Electione Gratiae Questiones Theosophicae* describes the determining mechanisms of the power of Will in this way:

The will is the 'mysterium magnum', the great mystery of all wonders and secrets, and yet it driveth forth itself, through the imagination of the desiring hunger, into substance. It is the original of nature; its desire maketh a representation; this representation is no other than the will of the desire, yet the desire maketh in the will such a substance as the will in itself is. The true 'Magia' is no substance, but the desiring spirit of substance; it is an unsubstantial matrix, and revealeth of manifesteth itself in the substance. The 'Magia' is a spirit, and the substance is its body. The 'Magia' is the greatest hidden secret, for it is above Nature; it maketh Nature according to the form of its will.

Another interesting definition is supplied by Evelyn Underhill in *Mysticism* (1930):

Magic in its uncorrupted form claims to be a practical, intellectual, highly individualistic science, working towards the declared end of enlarging the sphere on which the human will can work and obtaining experimental knowledge of the planes of being usually regarded as being transcendental.

Today we can define magic as a form of *active and aware mysticism*. I would like to discuss those aspects of magic knowledge that can be found among the basics of the discipline of 'Esoteric Physics'[39].

Aldous Huxley, citing the *Philosophia Perennis* of Leibniz, spoke of

A metaphysics that recognizes a divine consubstantial Reality in the world of things, lives and minds; it is a psychology that discovers in the soul something similar to divine Reality or even identical to it: an ethic which assigns Mankind as its final goal, the knowledge of the immanent and transcendent Foundation of all that which is.

Spiritual realization does not consist of reaching any particular certainty but of a continuous openness to change, of the continuous capacity to ask questions, to search, to grow and to renew oneself.

Man is a microcosm: that is, an image (concentrated around the point of consciousness) of the macrocosm, or Universe. This

---

[39] 'Esoteric Physics' is a term that I still use as a result of the experience I had in Damanhur up until 2004, during which I was the author of numerous essays on the subject. Having left that Community experience many years ago in order to pursue my own research in a freer and more authentic way that was closer to my feelings, I have taken it up again, integrated, compared and developed it in a direction all of my own – having discussed with many researchers in the broadest of multi-disciplinary contexts the exploration of what is an exceptionally vast subject.

theorem is guaranteed by the hylo-idealistic demonstration that the perceptible is an extension, or phantasm of the nervous system.

Aleister Crowley – Little Essays Towards Truth

According to all creation myths, the human being is a great primordial Consciousness that 'decides' to have a new experience by renouncing its oneness to reflect itself in a multiplicity of Form, renouncing all omniscience to explore unpredictability and therefore free will, to transform an *existential mechanism* into a *conscious process*. Mankind, forgets immortality to live in time and to experiment with transience and death, adventuring into the labyrinth of the possible to re-comprehend the cosmic sense of Self by means of life; our same life.

Form, worlds and every being are thus the pieces of a puzzle to be put back together according to a unitary and complete design that we conserve inside ourselves; that incorruptible memory of the All. We are Gods all intent on becoming human: we are humans in gestation.

Magic Orders and Systems

There is no other life besides this 'ordinary' life. Because men are incapable of living this ordinary life, they invent esoteric things. The mystery is here, the mystery is in the rocks, the mystery is in the trees, the mystery is in people, in you, in me, the mystery is in love, the mystery is in prayer. Ordinary life becomes extraordinary if you live it totally, fully. Avoid every esotericism. It is all foolishness. Eat breakfast and sleep well.

Osho

Osho's words are truly effective and liberating. Nevertheless, let's try to examine that particular way to knowledge and the realization of the self known as the *ritual and magic path* which is typical of our Hermetic and Western mystical tradition.

If we intend to interact with the mechanisms and the forces of reality inside and *outside* of us, not only at a personal level but also at a more complex level of collective egregors, there are only two possibilities: we either control or we are controlled.

To control we need to know exactly what we are doing and need to be able to act inside a method and a system of energetic reference that has to be searched for and rooted in the deepest parts of the pure and inviolable Self. We have to go beyond codified magic-ritual systems (be they traditional or recently activated), which can only be considered authentic and real if they educate and lead to that resolution, if they bring the individual closer to rather than further away from the inner self.

Over and above the intrinsic values of any esoteric-initiate Order, that traditionally has its own 'chrisms', the single individual should– and in many ways I would say *must* – be able to draw on his/her Self to construct their *own* system, when they have the capacity and power to do so.

All of this is necessary because, when connecting to 'external' forces, that are ready to transform themselves into larvae, predators or alien parasites, if they are not recognized as a part of us and eventually re-absorbed and commanded as such, just having a theoretical knowledge and being armed with goodwill is not enough. It is necessary to be knowledgeably and energetically prepared in order to sustain and confront such practices.

This 'energy', as long as it is not contained and expressed by our fully awakened consciousness, must be channelled through a *magic system* which is able to defend and correctly direct our action. But today it has become hard work to find a magic system which is not polluted by problematic spiritual, cultural and social contingences, in respect to its original values of purity and sacrality.

When we choose this kind of path, to truly obtain results, or at least the maximum efficacy, it is absolutely necessary to literally enter the *dimension of magic; to enter* into its logic and non-logic and prepare a system of references which is not only able to guide and contain us in our explorations but also the energy and power that we enter into relationship with.

Esotericism has to do with hidden truths, often knowingly kept secret, that can only be gathered through intuition or revelation and that elude all experimental verification. It is a particular kind of thought, irrational and intuitive, that aims at the union of nature and at the correspondences inside the latter and counts on the possibility of its unlimited transformation. Esotericism lives on the magic of the mysterious and thinks that it possesses a higher level of consciousness, that remains inaccessible to those who are not yet 'initiated' into the mysteries. With the reduction of the religious restraints that characterize our times, they increasingly carry out the function

185

of a substitute religion, which is resorted to for practical advice in order to deal with life: in the end though, this warps its nature as secret knowledge.

Erik Hornung

Whoever wishes to pursue their Path of Knowledge in this way needs to approach the environment that feels closest to their way of being and ethical values with great openness and availability but without ever losing contact with their own feelings, power of discernment and critical faculties and remaining faithful to their original aspirations. Remembering to listen to themselves and their own intuition and above all, individually re-establishing, in the privacy of meditation and concentration, contact with the true deeper Self in relation to the chosen context, its teachings and rituality. It is important not to confuse the ends with the means, gratification with true power (which is that over oneself), the knowledge of the mind with that over the heart. The only faithfulness that should be required is that you are always and only true to your Self.

Magic is often studied and practiced in the form of a mystic-magic exploration of the self and reality through initiate canons. Working with Orders of a Masonic, para-Masonic, Templar or neo-Pagan nature or even better Thelemic and is therefore aimed at a potential reformulation which is in tune with the paradigms of a New Era.

To those who are interested, other than inviting them to take an in-depth look at the differences between Magic, Spirituality and Rituality I would like to emphasize the following:

1) the need, above all, to *know* what it is you are talking about – and in that respect there will certainly be people who are more expert than you are

2) The absolute need to *renew* concepts and contents – in order to concentrate on your own research in that sense.

No matter how high the level of knowledge or magic is, or purports to be, if it is base and egoistic (which immediately excludes the concept and use of the term Magic for such practices), then it is aimed at the search for power and the satisfaction of personal ambition. In the same way, the more we search for, use and abuse external formula and *technologies*, the more we find ourselves faced with something that is completely deviated from the concept of Magic and even more so in respect to spirituality. When we work for the 'reawakening', or for the human and spiritual realization of ourselves by concentrating on our own search, it is important to renounce any ambition for personal power. This is often linked to the motivational dynamics of destructive groups and cults. In addition, ceremonial rituals and magic instruments must be seen merely as a temporary support for the inner process of recovery and the development of personal faculties and play an ever diminishing role in the awareness of inner power.

Wherever magic and ritual technology abounds and grows, churches, temples, annals and symbols, gods and sacraments, formula and dogma, priests and intercessors, there appears to be less 'consciousness' and 'soul'. It is almost as if it were the work of a demonic or *diabolic* entity designed to control us, to distance us from ourselves, to separate us from becoming aware and knowing what is real (diá-ballein = of he who divides)[40].

Wisdom does not lie in destroying idols but in never creating them in the first place.

Umberto Eco

Properly now because the time is right, it is important to take another look at techniques, methods, systems, correspondences and approaches relating to the Higher Self of the individual. We have to go beyond all forms of ceremony, of schemes, formulas, symbolism, of procedure and rituality and regain possession of a more direct and real sense of Self.

Let's dismantle those organizations, projects and mechanisms that in the light of the new paradigm seem to encumber rather than encourage Consciousness of the Self.

And personally cash in all the angels, demons and sigils, all the rites and all the Gods. Let's rewrite all the books and pension off all the grimoires, formularies and tables. Temples, vestments and magic instruments can be left to beautify museums.

---

[40] Obviously I am not criticizing spiritual discipline in itself, nor belittling the value of techniques and practices for sensitizing latent faculties: I am talking about the mental and spiritual manipulation that happens when these aspects are used, deviated and distorted, when money is made from them, making people dependent and exalting their egos. Religions, many spiritual groups, certainly cults, and for the most part the New Age have fallen into this trap, just as a certain magic re-evocation, significant and valid in itself, is in its turn distorted by operative keys that today I consider to be really antiquated if not bogus, ineffective if not deceptive.

This more personal approach has been defined as 'Krishnamurtism': it certainly derives from a profound admiration for Krishnamurti and for his discourse of 1929, in which he dissolved the *Order of the Star* at the moment in which thousands of Theosophists, having convened from all over the world were waiting for his formal teaching as 'Master of the World'[41].

This returns us to the individual, without too much mediation, ascending to the simplicity of Taoism, Zen and the origins of Buddhism. But also in the West (and not only in pre-Christian Gnosticism, Greek philosophy from before Socrates to Plato or buried in medieval mysticism) we find the same exhortation; for example, Louis-Claude de Saint-Martin (1743-1803), the inspiration behind the Martinist movement founded by Gérard Encausse (Papus) about eighty years later, writes in a letter to the Baron of Liebistorf on the 19th of June 1797:

The knowledge which formerly might be transmitted in writing depended on instructions which sometimes rested on certain mysterious practices and ceremonies, the value of which was more a matter of opinion and habit than of reality, and sometimes rested, in fact, on occult practices and spiritual operations, the details of which it would have been dangerous to transmit to the vulgar, or to ignorant and ill-intentioned men. The subject which engages us, not resting on such bases, is not exposed to similar dangers. The only initiation which I preach and seek with all the ardour of my soul, is that by which we may enter into the heart of God, and make God's heart enter into us,

---

[41] In 1929 during a world assembly of Theosophists at Ommen in Holland, Krishnamurti became the Krishnamurti that we know of today. I strongly recommend that you read the entire discourse in which he explains the heart of his message to the world: 'Truth is a Pathless Land'.
http://bernie.cncfamily.com/k_pathless.htm

there to form an indissoluble marriage, which will make us the friend, brother, and spouse of our divine Redeemer. There is no other mystery, to arrive at this holy initiation, than to go more and more down into the depths of our being and not let go till we can bring forth the living vivifying root, because then all the fruit which we ought to bear according to our kind, will be produced inside and outside of us.

Rituality has been subject to egoistic, emotive and deviate forces that are completely out of control and are linked to a search for image and power. In order to be recovered in its authentic form, it must be profoundly rooted in the Higher Self, or in that pure and incorruptible essence that is first and foremost to be rediscovered in ourselves. It is necessary that rituality remains a Path of great formative significance but, to recover its meaning and authentic worth it must be lived in great depth. It must be welcomed in private, in the silence of one's own intimacy, protected from inner and outer influences that can otherwise distance us from a true awareness of self and the meaning of our search. The individual has to be the protagonist: the point of convergence between this existence and the Absolute, with nothing allowed to come between: without mediators, allegories or symbols. There is no other Magic except will and love, the rite of life and meditation, thought and silence, art and conscious action.

The human being: is the only magic instrument, the only living rite and the new form of the Grail.

Let's focus everything on personal rediscovery, on a re-found ethic and on an active mysticism which is profoundly individual: one in which everyone regains possession of Consciousness and learns to define themselves with trust. Thus re-emanating their *own* Magic.

I apply and suggest this personal development; though without thinking or allowing myself to think, that it will prove easier this way. Just the opposite in fact.

The Kabbalah

The Kabbalah, the body of doctrine that forms the basis of Western mysticism, knew how to illustrate with great precision, minute detail and efficacy, the processes of creation that we looked at in the first chapter, describing both the creation of the world from high to low and implicitly indicating the path of re-ascension.

The Kabbalah is part of the esoteric tradition of Hebrew mysticism, in particular of the mystic thought which developed in Europe from the VII-VIII century. In Hebrew, *Qabbaláh is the act of receiving the Tradition*. However the Hebrew 'Kabbalah' should not be confused with the Kabbalah – or the Cabal – of Western tradition, which is directly inspired by it. The birth of the rise in Kabbalistic thought began with the publication of *The Book of Zohar* (splendour), in the XIII century. However, the essence of the elaboration of mystic doctrines relating to the secrets of creation probably derives from the work entitled *Sépher Yetziráh* of the VI or VII century.

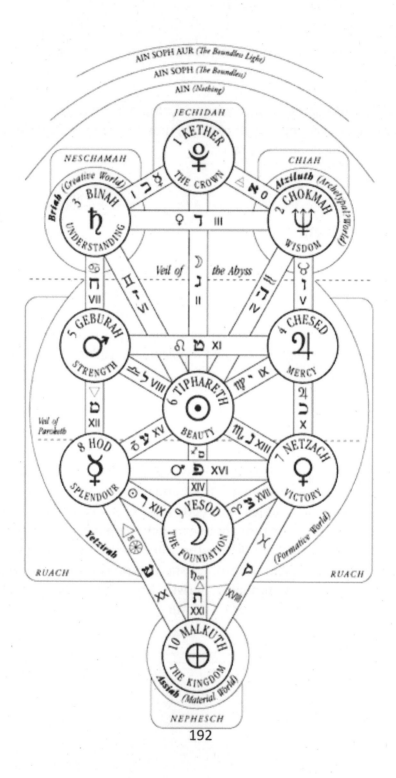

In the Sépher Yetziràh, which talks about the secret forces of the cosmos, we find the first mention of the term that will become central to successive speculation: the notion of the *sefiràh*. The *sephiroth* (plural) are the emanations of divine creative energy and are illustrated in the famous system of the Tree of Life (*Otz-Chiim*), now summarized in many different ways according to different traditions, uses, correspondences and methodology and employed in theoretical, mystical and operational-magic fields.

The sephiroth aim to describe the process according to which an infinite body emanates aspects of itself in a finite world. The Tree of the Sephiroth represents the sequence through which God 'contracts' itself in order to emanate its energy in the finite world and 'demonstrate' Its glory to the people'. The *contraction of God* lies at the heart of kabbalistic-esoteric speculation, as does the investigation of the Path for the re-expansion of Consciousness or the evolved identification of the creation with the creator.

The Tree of Life

Between the end of the XII and the beginning of the XIII century a vast amount of mystical literature appeared on the doctrine of the *sephiroth*; we can define them as the degrees of means by which God acts in the creation.

The Tree of Life constitutes the most noted and important synthesis of the teachings of the Hebrew Kabbalah. Traditionally it is an abstract and symbolic diagram comprising ten entities, called Sephiroth, positioned along three vertical parallel pillars: three on the left, three on the right and four in the centre.

In the centre of the diagram of the Tree of Life we find the column of equilibrium which, from Kether through Tipheret and Yesod, we reach Malkuth.

To the left and right of Kether two other columns branch off: those of Grace (or Mercy), through Chochmah, Chesed and Netzah; those of Severity rising again through Hod, Geburah and Binah.

The 10 Sephiroth are linked together by 22 pathways, associated with the letters of the Hebrew alphabet. According to different interpretations, working methods and authors, various possibilities have been presented of their possible associations and attributions, in particular those relating to the Major Arcana of the Tarot.

The spheres can also be distinguished as belonging to the *four worlds of the creation:* 'Atzilúth (world of the emanation, that includes the first three spheres), Beria (world of the creation, sphere of Geburah, Chesed and Tipheret), Yetzirà (world of Form, Hod, Netzach, Yesod) and 'Asiyá (world of production or manufacture, Malkuth). These names indicate the various types of influence of the sephiroth. The world of the Atzilut, which is the closest to God, is ruled by exclusively immaterial forces: the material component increases as distance from the Emanator is slowly increased. We could associate the four worlds to the four principal phases of re-evolution: material-life-thought-consciousness.

The *sephiroth* have to be perceived through contemplation and the study of cosmic correspondences. In fact all the different parts of the cosmos have correspondences in the Kabbalistic system: Tipheret is the Sun, Yesod the Moon, Malkuth the Earth and so on. The 22 pathways are also associated with the letters of the Hebrew alphabet, the Tarot, the signs of the Zodiac, the planets and the elements and as a consequence with plants, stones, colours and alchemical phases. Many tables of correspondences exist each relating to different traditions and working methods. Among the most celebrated are the attributes elaborated by Eliphas Levi, which were later revisited by important Orders such as the Golden Dawn, the Ordo Templis Orientis (OTO), the Argenteum Astrum (A.A.) and others. Even today they still use the Tree of Life as their principal system of reference.

The Kabbalah and Hermeticism

Just as in many traditions, the manifestations of the creation for the Hebrews are to be found in their alphabet: in the sign that individuates each one, in their pronunciation and in their corresponding number. These letters, associated to the 22 pathways of the Kabbalistic tree, can be likewise associated to the 22 cards of the Major Arcana of the Tarot, depending on the type of logic adopted.

Gematria is the numerological study of the written word in the Hebrew language and it is an analytical method used for interpreting sacred texts. It is based on the fact that every word expressed in the Hebrew alphabet can be associated with a number obtained by adding the numerical values of each letter used. The words and the phrases that add up to the same value are connected to each other in some way. A Greek Kabbalah also exists: which celebrates, for example, the number 93, which has the same value according to Gematria as the words

Thelema and Agape, literally meaning Will with Love, the spiritual values of reference, recovered and adopted by modern initiate disciplines that precisely identify with the so called *Current 93*, which in many ways and non-exclusively has inspired the Italian, 'Centro Studi Ascensione 93'[42].

The art of the *notariqón* however, allows one to discover words hidden inside other words.

In the twelfth century *Séfer ha-Zóhar* alchemical notes can already be found linked to the symbolism of the sephiroth and the transmutation of metals. The seven kinds of gold mentioned in the traditions become a metaphor of the seven lower sephiroth and therefore the seven planets, the seven ages of Man, our personalities or the levels to which every personality has to ascend in order to perfect itself. Other traditions, or other ways of using the Kabbalistic system, use the number 12 in order to work with the same associations.

In Western tradition, the Kabbalah represents the meeting point between all aspects of esoteric experience: Magic, Gnosticism, Orphism, etc. It borrows ideas from the mystical

---

[42] The 'Centro Studi Ascensione 93' is an **Italian** study group for discussion and research which I founded in 2005 and consists of free researchers in the field of human evolution, spirituality and frontier sciences. Without hierarchies and dogmatism, it is an observatory, a container for resources and a workshop for shared experiences. The research and experimentation is inspired by the spiritual, ritual, mystic and esoteric traditions of the East and West, by the Gnosis of all times and places as well as modern developments in science and human knowledge, for the development of new approaches and subject matter. The group operates autonomously and believes in self-determination and in individual responsibility as the key to personal and collective growth. It is mostly an online portal, but nevertheless presents and develops its own cultural initiatives through Conferences, Seminars and Study Groups in many Italian cities.

approach of the Hebrew Kabbalah but mostly avoids the religious confines of that experience.

It is not easy to establish a historical beginning for this form of mysticism, because it can be traced back to a continuous exchange between the mystical world of the Hebrews and other esoteric cultures, among which, those of the lands of Egypt and Babylon.

For an introduction to the modern Kabbalah reference is usually made to the book, *The Mystical Qabalah* of Dion Fortune or to the essays of Israel Regardie.
Historically the beginning of the Hermetic Kabbalah can be linked to the English society of the Golden Dawn, among whose founders were Samuel Liddel MacGregor Mathers and William Wynn Westcott. They created a system in which the fundamental elements of Western tradition are harmonized under the umbrella of the Tree of Life.

Aleister Crowley gives the following definition of the Kabbalah:

(a). A language fitted to describe certain classes of phenomena, and to express certain classes of ideas which escape regular phraseology. You might as well object to the technical terminology of chemistry.

(b). An unsectarian and elastic terminology by means of which it is possible to equate the mental processes of people apparently diverse owing to the constraint imposed upon them by the peculiarities of their literary expression. You might as well object to a lexicon, or a treatise on comparative religion.

(c). A system of symbolism which enables thinkers to formulate their ideas with complete precision, and to find simple

expression for complex thoughts, especially such as include previously disconnected orders of conception. You might as well object to algebraic symbols.

(d). An instrument for interpreting symbols whose meaning has become obscure, forgotten or misunderstood by establishing a necessary connection between the essence of forms, sounds, simple ideas (such as number) and their spiritual, moral, or intellectual equivalents. You might as well object to interpreting ancient art by consideration of beauty as determined by physiological facts.

(e). A system of classification of omniform ideas so as to enable the mind to increase its vocabulary of thoughts and facts through organizing and correlating them. You might as well object to the mnemonic value of Arabic modifications of roots.

(f). An instrument for proceeding from the known to the unknown on similar principles to those of mathematics. You might as well object to the use of i, x^4, etc.

(g). A system of criteria by which the truth of correspondences may be tested with a view to criticizing new discoveries in the light of their coherence with the whole body of truth. You might as well object to judging character and status by educational and social convention.

The current interest in the Kabbalah arises from its subtle psychological references that, according to its enthusiasts makes an optimum instrument for reflection on, and investigation into, the human soul.

The Ten Sephiroth

The Sephiroth are:

- Kether (crown), the highest and closest to the Absolute
- Binah (science or knowledge) and Chochmah (wisdom)
- Gheburáh (strength) and Chesed (compassion or pity)
- Tipheret (beauty)
- Hod (glory) and Netzah (eternity or victory)
- Yesod (foundation or founding)
- Malkuth (kingdom), the material world.

These are the names most frequently used. Sometimes Gheburah is characterized in *Din* (justice) and *Pachad* (fear), Chesed can be called *Ghedulláh* (greatness), Tipheret *Rakhamím* (compassion)[43].

An 'eleventh' Sephira exists: *Da'at*, the hidden sephira, which is positioned between Binah, Chokmah and Chesed and represents the abyss between Man and the Absolute. Astrologically it is associated with the star Sirius, and consequently to Seth and all the important representations that refer to it.

It is also possible to use personal constructions to help focus oneself by means of the Kabbalah.

---

[43] For a more in-depth look at the Magic Kabbalah I recommend 'The Tree of Life' and *A Garden of Pomegranates* by Israel Regardie and, for enthusiasts, I suggest the indispensable reference, *Kabbalah* by Gersholm Scholem.

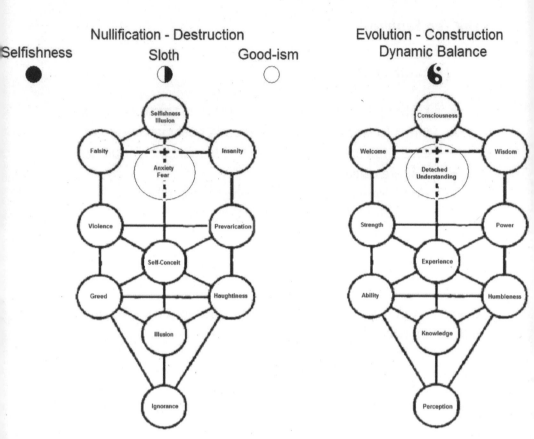

The construction of additional hypotheses and systems of interpretation of the self through further elaboration of this valid method is the best instrument of self-analysis in existence. It can be considered even more so, if regarded in all its correspondences on the macro and micro-cosmic plane and compared with other systems of analysis such as alchemical transmutations, the system of the chakra and the more modern 'enneagram', adopted for decades by certain schools of the 'Fourth Way'[44] (but with much more ancient origins).

---

[44] 'The Fourth Way' is a system which was introduced at the beginning of the last century by George I. Gurdjieff to reach a real and complete development of the individual. The name 'Fourth Way' is used to

Gods in Exile

Esoteric chronicles tell of a Golden Age and of a very complex and evolved human being: they speak of giants, of long-lived beings with bodies which are much more ethereal than ours of today. Ideally our incarnation should happen in a dimensional state between the Absolute and the material world. Instead we have fallen down into a level of reality which is a long way away from the source.

Leaving aside all the non-esoteric theories that sustain we are the result of a system of hybridization on the part of gods/cosmic aliens; on theoretical, eschatological and ontological planes, we have to admit that we have truly 'fallen' into the third dimension. Whether it is part of the original plan or the consequence of errors or difficulties encountered along the road matters very little. The fact is, this is the condition we are in. We live in a restricted and illusory reality that our mind is continuously redefining. A conventional reality reprocessed by our brain, totally fictitious and without purpose, springing from reduced, incomplete mental and sensorial perceptions. It is extremely restricted, manipulated and limited in respect to our *status*, which in some way or other or for some reason we have lost. However, it is this experience that we have been

---

differentiate the system from others that Gurdjieff described in relation to specific work on the human being: The 'Way of the Fakir', is expressed through the use of the body to reach a higher level of awareness. The 'Way of the Monk', is expressed through the use of emotion, as in faith and 'mystic rapture'. The 'Way of the Yogi', is the use of intellectual parts to achieve consciousness. The Fourth Way is founded on the balanced use of all the functions through their simultaneous development. Gurdjieff emphasizes the need for holistic development in order to reach the objective of a completed individual.

called upon to live and it is from this that we have to re-emerge.

Using a simile, we could compare our present relationship with the Real to the movement of an octopus which, with its tentacles, explores the rocks and the depths of the sea. Each tentacle is one of our 'incarnations' (our many lives) and as human beings we are conscious of our unity, that is, of being the octopus that towers over everything. Now, imagine that the octopus loses that awareness of itself and identifies only with one tentacle at a time (what we consider to be our present identity, seen as the incarnation we are aware of now, as our 'life'), and that particular tentacle clinging to the rocks turns to stone: having penetrated so far into the rock it totally identifies with it. The meaning of the comparison is precisely this: we have forgotten that we are the whole octopus and above all we are 'mineralized' or petrified – according to alchemical jargon - in matter, in the world of materialism.

We are petrified from a mental, psychic and physical point of view because materialism, or the loss of natural sensitivity, stops us perceiving and feeling and therefore of elaborating and understanding. The monks initiated into the Hermetic Tradition, knew how to see a living consciousness in everything that exists.

Mario Balocco – La Magia nei Monasteri

Our present Consciousness only allows us a limited vision of reality, like that of a child raised by monkeys or amidst the horrors of war, but which is nevertheless seen as 'normal'.

The 'real fall' therefore does not rest so much in the incarnation as in the successive loss of identity and degeneration into the material.

Our identity should already be, as it were, in *Tipheret* but instead we are 'monkeys', unfledged bipeds and confused hominids.

On the Kabbalistic Tree of Life we could illustrate the situation with the image shown on the next page.

Applying the terms of the Kabbalah to this hypothesis we can therefore suppose that our role as a bridge-Form, because of its nature, should already position us in Tipheret, instead however, we have 'fallen' through the veil of illusion (*Yesod*), into Malkuth, by identifying with the material world and becoming dense and corporeal. In practice *mineralizing* ourselves inside the material world rather than conserving our spiritual position. From here that 'derived creation', that surrogate of reality which is our current pseudo- existence is not dissimilar to that of *Golem*: a foolish automaton (as defined by Hasidic Judaism). In this scenario we should also consider the history or perhaps half-history that is related by ancient and modern esoteric chronicles. They describe the current earth-being as the result of a sort of 'derived creation' on the part of ultra-dimensional alien races, interested in generating or manipulating living beings in order to exploit them for their labour; farm them as psychic nourishment or else perform 'genetic' or bio-spiritual experiments on them[45].

Whether our fall is of a spiritual origin, which means it has always been part of the same game, or has become part of a

---

[45] Theses which I take note, of but which I personally do not feel it is necessary to take a position on.

cosmic game beyond the expectations of eventual alien or divine creators, in both cases our present condition derives from tremendous confusion about 'who we are' and therefore, what are or have become, the aims of our existence. This is why the first objective of any esoteric school should be to enter into contact with the true Self and reposition the barycentre of our identity in it. In *Tipheret* to be precise.

Evolution should imply above all the re-appropriation of our original nature, a recovery from handicap and a return to what we are (teshuvà), so that we can finally evolve ourselves and reality to not only a level of major awareness but also of greater energy and psycho-physical power.
Instead, Man behaves like a diver who has fainted in his diving suit, one that is decidedly rusty and in a bad way with several portholes (senses) closed or out of focus, casually wandering around in a clumsy way, swayed by the currents of a reality that he has lost consciousness of and no longer controls.

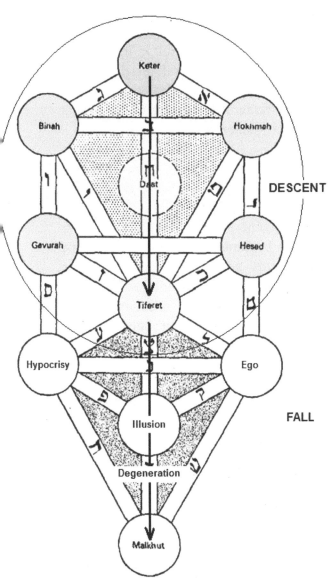

DESCENT Our regular incarnation from Kether to Tipheret which is the level of reality we belong to as a bridge-Form between the material and the spiritual.

But, for a series of reasons we dropped down by identifying ourselves in Malkut and moving the 'centre of mass' of our identity into matter, thus becoming lost in the illusion.

FALL

If from Tipheret the door to re-ascending is at the level of Da'at, or the temptaion of the superior ego, then from Malkut we are caught up in the molasses of the illusion. The door to ascension lies in Yesod by just recovering our proper identity. From Yesod we will finally be able to redeem the awareness of who-we-are and the real reality we are here to experience. The true nature of our evolutionary mission will then become obvious.

Today, the rather inflated concept of enlightenment has to separate itself from the purely mental, ethereal and spiritual definition of the idea – which is just as abstract as the Western mind – and recover the original meaning of metamorphosis and transfiguration, or transubstantiation, above all in its material sense. It is most of all a physical process: an ontological mutation of the human Form. In the end it is not the soul that has to be conquered but the body. It is not the Absolute that we have to understand but this reality.

I definitely agree with Thomas Moore who insisted on saying that if spiritual masters and the community were to seriously consider this point, spirituality would lose its sentimental idealism and appeal to intelligent people... Nobody imagines that spirituality is the way to become an ordinary person, one who confronts banal problems and consequently lives an ordinary life. Many people attracted by the spirit find it difficult to be simple human beings, and renounce practical intelligence in the name of idealistic visions. This 'inflated' behaviour can take over people and daze them.

In order to do this, first of all we have to recalibrate all our sensorial and mental filters: we live in a reality deformed by flawed lenses. Although it is here (and from here) that we have to process reality, without making a fuss about being gods again and wanting to perform miracles: in the end we have come here to conquest *this* 'reality'.

The 'work' that needs to be done is primarily on ourselves: on the lenses of our consciousness and our psycho-bio-physical vehicle. To achieve what does not need theoretical reasoning, ideas and mentalism as its reference, nor the fashions of the New Age. We need instead to practice observation, attention, and consciously relate to life, events, people and things without worrying too much about notions of enlightenment.

We have to start with ourselves: it is *from here*, from this material and mental molasses that all *real* evolution blooms. The Angels, the Masters and the Gods need us much more than we will ever need them!

Thoughts on Alchemy

Voarchadumia, ars distincta ab Archimia et Sophia is the title of a work published by Giovanni Agostino Pantheo in 1530 in which the author attempts to create some order amongst various interpretations of the methods and aims of Alchemy. In 1518, Pantheo published *Ars transmutationis metallicae* and he was perhaps the first to relate the Alchemical Work (*Cabalisticum archimicae artis magisterium*) to the Kabbalah, by introducing the Hebrew names of the Tetragrammaton and *Gematria* into his treatises. With the term *Voarchadumia* he firmly specifies the difference between Alchemy, a term which refers to the ignorant and fraudulent and *Archemy* (from *archè* = principle and *mia* = one, therefore 'the principle of unity') namely, the True Art of the Transmutation of Metals and the *Elixir of Life*.

This treatise on 'spiritual 'metallurgy which inspired the greatest Hermeticists and alchemists of the epoch, narrates that Voarchadumia was also a Hermetic and Rosicrucian Society (probably of Portuguese origin though its most important general quarter was to be found in Venice). Custodian not only of esoteric mysteries and scientific knowledge (then heretical) but also practices of an alchemical, magic and tantric nature, it interwove occult relationships between Hermeticists and Scientists. It was often forced to remain hidden, along with the powerful of the time, in order to preserve and develop knowledge because of the obscurantism of the Church and the narrow mindedness of Aristotelian thinkers. Certainly the Jesuits, just as in the case of the Illuminati of Bavaria[46], sought, in every way possible, to obstruct these forms of spiritual search, free experimentation and circulation of knowledge. They even went so far as to produce counterfeit documents and certificates, many of which today, for example, are waved around as proof of the existence of a connection between the

---

[46] The Illuminati or to be more precise the Order of the Illuminati, is the name of a secret Bavarian society of the XVIII century. The name has been associated, for the most part wrongly, with numerous secret societies of occult origin. The Order of the Illuminati was founded in Ingolstadt (Germany) in 1776 by Johann Adam Weishaupt (1748-1830). At the beginning its members were just university students, with the declared intent of promoting the works of 'Lumi' inside the state of Bavaria, which prohibited many such writings. In reality, the thought of Adam Weishaupt which was much more occult, sustained that "Every man is capable of finding the Inner Light inside of himself... becomes equal to Jesus, that is Man-King...". The society was formed as an alternative to the newly born German Masonry, maintaining its character of secrecy and hierarchical divisions on the basis of initiation. According to the judicial deposition of Professor Renner during the legal proceedings in Bavaria: "The Order of the Illuminati should be clearly distinguished from that of the Freemasons. But this difference is not recognized by simple Freemasons, neither by new initiates of the Minervale Grade. The Illuminati no longer fear to be recognized by this name". From the Middle Ages to modern times various organizations have defined themselves as the 'Illuminati' for example: the Confraternity of the Free Spirit, the Rosicrucians, the Alumbrados, the Illuminés, the Martinists and the Palladists.
From the 1800's, especially in the field of conspiracy theories, a widespread socio-pathological phenomenon for a couple of centuries if not more, the term 'Illuminati' has been generally associated with followers of secret societies inspired by occult a/o globalist ideas, independent of whether they were in fact really correlated to the Order of the Illuminati: Skull & Bones, Round Table, Pilgrim Society, Fabian Society, Royal Institute of International Affairs, Council on Foreign Relations, Bohemian Club, Bilderberg Group, the Trilateral Commission, the Club of Rome, the Carnegie Foundation, the Rockefeller Foundation etc.

Bavarian Illuminati and the 'Illuminati' of conspiracy theorists, or those of the New World Order and its mysterious and powerful *elite*, behind which hide notorious alien hierarchies and ancestral families of hybrid terrestrials.

Without negating the existence of large scale political-economical influence, we need to neatly distance ourselves from conspiracy theories as they are presented today (most of all those with a disputable historical basis, which in turn trigger likewise disputable 'Evemeristic' reconstructions[47] of myths and human archetypes). Unfortunately, today the term Illuminati is now mostly used to definitively indicate this true or purportedly true global *elite*.

The *Voarchadumia* also seems to be linked with the so called 'Hungarian Lodge' (in its turn linked to the 'Himalayan Lodge') as well as a mysterious Secret Society operating in the XVI and XVII centuries in Europe, also noted in 1470 as 'The Fog' or the 'Angelic Society'.

Such derivations lead back to more archaic fraternities like that of the (mythical) Naacal, however we must also bear in mind that all initiate societies seek to trace their origins back in time, sometimes alleging outlandish pseudo-historic concatenations to ancient Egypt, Atlantis and so on, rather than to Chaldean priests. Even though their historical attempts may prove to be inadequate, it is important to consider the symbolic and archetypical connections they have with such values at a spiritual level of elective affinities and magic revival.

---

[47] Evemerism was a position on the philosophy of religion held by Evemero, historian and philosopher of the Hellenistic age who sustained that the gods represent deified human subjects.

The myth arising around this Rosicrucian Order with its bizarre name, talks of a document known as the *Protocol of the Elders of Caldeirão,* of Atlantean origins which is kept in the pyramids of Giza. The writings supposedly hand down the traditions of Agartha, a kingdom inside the Earth's core governed by a 'King of the World', whose access is guarded by ethereal hyperborean guardians in strict alliance with the grand Masters such as: Hermes Trismegistus, John Dee, Nicolas Flamel, Cagliostro, Saint-Germain and therefore M.me Blavatsky etc. Members of the Voarchadumia, included many artists, philosophers, scientists and Renaissance alchemists, the same John Dee (the Order widely used the method of evocation outlined in the *'Keys of Enoch'*), Giordano Bruno, Giorgione, Francesco Colonna and perhaps Galileo.

There exists an Alchemy of Living Forces, an Alchemy of Spent Forces and a series of successive classifications (Tantra, Alchemy of Characters, Alchèmy of the People, Alchemy of Metals, Genetic Alchemy, Spagyrical, Temporal and so on).

In the *Horusian* tradition, the term 'Spent Forces' is used to describe the energies closed inside minerals, in the Earth, Air, Water and Fire - even though the latter possesses peculiar characteristics that distinguish it from other 'spent' elements. –

If material *Form* is individuated into basic elements (although this is described in very different terms in Eastern Alchemy), the distinctive parameters for all planes of existence are:

- The number of dimensions
- The level of density
- The temporal direction

It is clear how, at a certain level, Alchemy fuses with Esoteric Physics and the latter with Magic and therefore mysticism: the distinctions between such disciplines however, should only be seen as purely conventional and didactically useful.

All the forces that derive from life are 'Living Forces', those that originate from living, human, animal and vegetable Form, or of a subtle or divine nature.

'Living Forces' contain vital essence, the intrinsic quality of living Form, the emotional element, the function or specific ability, or else the particular state of consciousness expressed in a given moment, represented and supported by a *simulacrum* (witness) that can also be – but not necessarily – an animal, a plant or its parts.

The fundamental precepts of Alchemy are: To Know - To Dare - To Want -To Be Silent.

The Alchemist investigates and evolves him/herself by means of the world; investigates and evolves the world by means of him/herself. The true aim of Alchemy is in fact to realize the Complete Human Being or to reassemble the Primordial Androgen. The whole of the alchemical process is a *ritual* and it is necessary to be 'initiated': The Esoteric Order is in its turn an alchemical *Atanor* (crucible) of Living Forces.

The interdisciplinary investigation into the extraordinary relationship between alchemical allegory and the psychology of the inner self can be found in the admirable work of Carl. G. Jung. On this occasion it is important to know that in every pure *alchemical element*, expediently dealt with and conserved, precise equilibriums and priorities of *derivative laws* are combined in a fixed and immutable composition.

Knowing the specific dominances, in every element, the alchemist is able to indirectly manipulate the fundamental laws of our world by using alchemical elements, rather than operating directly on the time matrices which is the goal of Magic - although at a higher level – be it alchemical or magic/realizational. This relationship with reality is searched for inside the self, where the functions of the world are recognized as expressions of one's own working Consciousness.

By Alchemy we are talking about operating on 'maya', of finding the correspondences for moving – by means of the essences – the fundamental constituents of the forces of Nature, while with Alchemy and Magick – the term used by Crowley to distinguish this high level of Magic from its lower and more distorted expressions – we explore the reflections of our world/consciousness on the real and vice versa.

When dealing with Alchemy it is necessary to mention an important concept that is often neglected: the Shadow element.

In this world where we forget
We are shadows of who we are,
And the real actions we perform
In the other world, where we live as souls,
Are here wry grins and appearances.

Fernando Pessoa

The existence of 'something' is always preceded by the idea of its absence, or else by its non-existence. After all, in our daily lives is it not true to say that we only realize the value of something when it is missing?

When a universe is born a counter universe, is also born as compensation $(0 = (+1) + (-1))$: the shadow universe, or 'universe B'. It has nothing to do with anti-matter and is a profound and complete antithesis: an immaterial universe.

In fact, from the processes of the cosmic creation, described in the first chapter, the manifestation of the universe of Form not only emanates at various levels and existential planes, but also its 'shadow': a *counter-universe* whose door of access is represented on the Tree of Life, by the mysterious and controversial sphere of *Daath*. There we find the point of union (and separation) not between mass and energy, but between the Absolute and the Universe, between Empty and Full, between Creator and Creation, between Reality and Illusion, between Knowledge and the Abyss.

In the same way, when we 'create' an element in alchemical operations, we 'extract' it from the All and, as compensation, the corresponding counter-element is generated in the *shadow* universe.

For example, in Hebrew tradition, revived and re-elaborated by modern esoteric schools of thought, the Kabbalistic Tree of Life, with its Sephiroth, represents the universe as luminous and manifest. But another universe also exists, that of the shadowy and destructive Qliphoth: the dark side of that tradition.

The Alchemist has to manage both sides of reality harmoniously and elevate him/herself above duality and appearances.

The Tattwa

The principal meditative techniques for exploring traditional alchemical elements usually envisage the use of the Tattwa (in particular the meditation known as *Tattwa Shuddhi*, an original technique re-elaborated in the West by the Hermetic Order of the Golden Dawn).

In Eastern traditions the archetypical elements of the creation of the macrocosm – Air, Earth, Fire, Water and Ether – are also to be found in the microcosm, or human being, precisely in the form of the Tattwa.

Discovering, purifying and re-ordering these elements in yourself by means of meditation, is working on the Tattwa: it is the first phase of many initiate disciplines.

The Tattwa, corresponding to the 5 elements (even though schools exist that include another 2 or 3 hidden and reserved for advanced techniques), interact with one another and, by doing so, provoke changes in the universe at both micro and macro levels.

For this reason in tantric tradition, the sequence of the manifestation of the creation is described as follows: basically it is absolute consciousness (Brahman) from which Prana, or Shakti emanates and from which, in its turn, the cosmic mind also emanates and consequently the five elements. Every Tattwa is a certain vibrational level of Prana (the breath, or the universal vital energy, similar to light which contains all colours); every Tattwa, being a vibrational level of Prana, is symbolized by a different colour.

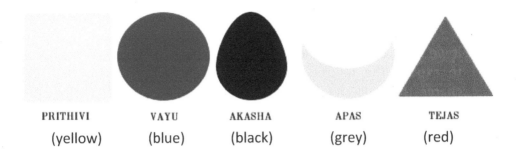

PRITHIVI	VAYU	AKASHA	APAS	TEJAS
(yellow)	(blue)	(black)	(grey)	(red)

The five Tattwa are: Akash, the principle of Ether; Vayu, the etheric principle of Air; Tehas, the etheric principle of Fire; Prithvi, the etheric principle of the element Earth and finally Apas, the etheric principle of Water.

Senses, Emotions and Faculties

If we want to raise the level of our perspective, it is necessary to expand the references of our perceptions. Normally we charge the body, its sensations and the physical senses with supplying the basic and definitive indications for orienting ourselves on the material plane and in each case they take their references from mental processes. But there is nothing *rational* about it: the processing actually happens in the unconscious and it is the mind that helps us to justify – with the semblance of logic – our actions, behaviour and choices. But, if we want to get closer to our essence and become more aware, we have to place other references alongside those of the body and consider them not only trustworthy, but even more so than the picture we habitually use as a reference. These additional references are the emotions when they function as 'senses'.

If we learn to listen to ourselves, to *listen* to our emotions in an increasingly direct and aware manner, to be attentive witnesses to our sensations and what we 'feel', we can not only acquire a greater consciousness of ourselves and others but activate a sort of 'radar' which proves much more precious than the ordinary senses. It can supply us with precise and meaningful information about ourselves, the world around us, the choices we need to make and our evolutionary path.

Looking at it in these terms, we can affirm that spiritual evolution is above all the evolution of human feelings, the true patrimony of a growing consciousness.

We need however, to distinguish between emotivity and emotion: the first usually commands us by overwhelming us, while the second, on the contrary, allows us to assume mastery over ourselves and our impulses, sustains the development of our consciousness and helps us to extract that 'added value' from life, things, events and relationships with others.

With the emotions we construct a bridge towards the Real and a path to the development of higher faculties.

If the senses are the perceptive organs of the body and the material plane, then the emotions are the 'senses of the soul', or the sense organs of our personalities, soul, and a higher and more expansive level of reality: one that is more allied to our real plane of existence as a bridge-Form between the material world and the spirit.

Certainly we are talking about undertaking an attentive and assiduous task, to observe ourselves in order to learn to feel, recognize and guide our own emotions and transform them into true 'sense organs'. The education of 'feeling', of listening to our emotions and using them as existential feedback allows them to be used as a measure of energy and personal growth and even as 'ethical indicators'.

Let's look at an example which begins with the technical experience of extending the faculties and then extends that concept to everyday life.
We have already talked about the 'sense of dream', as an inner faculty which allows us to achieve greater awareness of our being and our reality: a reality, which we acknowledge as a well-devised and rather convincing kind of dream from which we have to awaken. Therefore, the sense of dream is a subtle and spiritual faculty for exploring 'other' states of reality but above all for finally 'seeing' what our reality really is, or could be, beyond the restrictive and distorting filters of the mind (or at least that which our mind has become). The organs of the sense of dream are our own emotions.

But be careful: we are not talking about a confused emotivity that is out of control but a conscious 'feeling'. The emotions then become a reference for orienting ourselves not only in oneiric and astral explorations but also – and above all – for guiding us on our evolutionary journey through everyday life.

When we do exercises to recover the 'sense of dream' we need to work on two fronts:

1. Carry out the integration of our masculine and feminine alchemical components, a necessary requisite in order to transcend the restrictions and the duality of our habitual mental patterns and therefore to process perceptions in an integrated and unitary form.

2. Learn to use the emotions as organs for the perception of reality and indicators of vital and spiritual energy, to identify deficiencies that could be compensated for by adopting a more precise astuteness, in ethical and behavioural terms, during the course of our everyday life.

Let's look at the following table: a conventional and generalized instrument, valid in didactic terms, which provides an example of what needs to be understood and processed on an individual level. Please note that each *derivative law*, *sephira* and *chakra* (to be considered with all the other correspondences that such references imply) is associated with an emotion, in its positive and negative form.

Universal Functions	Sephiroth	Chakra	Emotions		Faculties	Mantra	Attitude	Buddhism	Ashtanga Yoga
			Positive	Negative					
Frequency	Malkuth	coccyx	happiness	unhappiness	dimensions/aura	A	action	right action	Yama
Interaction	Yesod	genitals	security	insecurity	memory	E1	continuity-coherence	right mindfulness	Nyama
Sacred Geometry	Hod/Netzach	plexus	joy	suffering	mind	E2	depth	right concentration	Asana
anent Consciousness	Tipheret	heart	love	hate	intent	O1	welcome-availability	right intention	Pranayama
Correspondence	Geburah/Chesed	throat	gaiety	sadness	para-telepathy	O2	exploration-movement	right effort	Pratyahara
Synchronicity	Daath	"mobile"	completeness	defeat	emotions	IAOUE-EUOAI	art-creativity	right speech	Dharana
Chaos	Binah/Chockmah	3rd eye	serenity	restlessness	dream	U	renovation-adaptability	right livelihood	Dyana
Complexity	Kether	crown	beatitude	anguish	consciousness	I	sharing-generation	right view	Samadhi

When we use dream at that level, or we are in the phase of astral projection, we need to be aware of the emotion that we are feeling.

This is not the right place to go into detail about the techniques of dreaming or out of the body journeys, nevertheless I would like to underline the role that the emotions play during our meditations and explorations. The type of emotion experienced furnishes indications regarding the dimension being explored. The fact that it is perceived in positive or negative terms indicates the balance, or lack of it – or disharmony – of a certain type of energy in ourselves. Deficiencies, which can be resolved by paying attention to certain aspects of our behaviour in everyday life. Those who are on a spiritual path and inner search – headed by different schools of Western or Eastern origin – will probably wish to note, in a more attentive manner, the peculiar association of ideas and concepts that are proposed[48].

Other than working with the sense of dream it is also possible to extend the use of this method to our everyday lives. This means, through the exercise of self-observation and

---

[48] A more in-depth look at the use of these techniques and the references mentioned in the table can be more efficaciously supplied during the meetings and public conferences that I often hold to explore such subjects.

remembering the self: learning to listen to and recognize the emotions in order to transform them into an appropriate weight and therefore adopt the necessary behavioural skills that take into account, for example, the *sephira* rather than the *chakra* corresponding to any negative emotion experienced. This is where a conscious relationship with reality becomes a continuous feedback for personal work.

For example, I can ask myself this question: during a dream, or when I wake up, or in a given moment of my day – without there seeming to be any direct cause – does a sense of sadness prevail?[49]

According to this method[50] I find myself in the throat chakra, in the dimensions of Geburah and Chesed, or in the workings of 'correspondence' in which my inner faculties coincide with a 'sense of exchange' or an emotive and para-telepathic relationship with others.

Therefore, the behaviour that we need to work on relates to our capacity to move and explore outside of recognized patterns. It calls for a change in the logic necessary for adaptation, to move in an active way to explore new possibilities in the context of relations with others and to force ourselves to adopt a more evolved level of interaction. Reflections are integrated by working on the particular sephiroth and chakra indicated and by exploring the elements and their relative psycho-physical and spiritual functions. Our

---

[49] In order to affirm this, it is necessary to have already done many exercises and trials and acquired a certain familiarity in recognizing one's own emotions: it therefore implies a dedication to meditation practices and a minute observation of the self.

[50] This is simply a method, an instrument, a hypothesis for work that should be investigated and explored with intelligence and a capacity to adapt and apply oneself, without forgetting the collective archetypes which were used in order to generate the initial table.

emotions, consciously born and guided are truly the senses of our soul and the instruments of our spirituality. They 'give meaning to things' and construct a bridge between the human and the divine, between the immanent and the transcendent and between our senses and our spiritual faculties. We can achieve all this through practices applied to our everyday lives.

The 'spiritual' plane in itself does not exist, except as the correct expression of every existential level and its integration with others in relation to the concept of Consciousness.

Ritual, Dream and Ecstasy

In the film *The Thirteenth Floor* (by Josef Rusnak, 1999) a multi-level reality is presented: every lower universe is a presented as a sort of three-dimensional video game – that nevertheless possesses its own autonomy and therefore its own relative 'intelligent' reality – in which the people of a higher universe play and have created through the dominion of avatars. In the film the 'first reality' is also shown, the one that created the first simulation in which certain 'people' created a second simulation and so on. All the 'people' of each simulation – at every level – are 'alive', intelligent, sentient: they are perfectly programmed software. However, some of them begin to understand and rebel. One of them, the protagonist, who is living in an intermediate reality and plays with successive simulations, certainly does not think he is living in or is in turn a simulation impossessed from time to time by a player of a higher level. In a spectacular manner, a little like *The Truman Show*, he discovers the truth about his 'world' and his conditions and achieves the impossible feat: his 'mind' manages to scale the preceding levels to impossess the controller of the first reality.

He manages to ascend not from the level of reality he belongs to but by paradoxically going down into the lower simulations to then trigger a process of return by 'launching' himself not to the height of his own reality but into the preceding ones to arrive at the first, the true original one.

This movie, which is based on a science-fiction novel, is of great interest because it is one of the first that explicitly presents the model of virtual realities (... yes, Plato had already done it with his 'myth of the cave').

The film makes one think that our return towards *true reality*, which in fact we do not actually know, might not necessarily happen by aiming directly for it but could happen as the result of an 'elastic' effect achieved by launching into the depths of ourselves, perhaps into the depths of our own illusion and its under-programming. Consciously.

We exist in this Reality not to live in a state of perfection, to be divine and perform miracles but to be 'humans' and manoeuvre ourselves more or less convulsively, in this very contradictory, complex and at times difficult, if not bizarre, environment.

The investigation of the self, or if we prefer religion, spirituality, mysticism, magic, uses instruments that do not, in effect, aim at the higher destination but instead increase the illusion into which we have fallen. They create further under-programmes in which, having once recognized our *status* and re-awoken, we can re-qualify not only for the level we started out from but if we are ready to do so, for a higher reality.

The state of consciousness that allows each one of us to release ourselves from our present reality and throw ourselves into the depths - through abstinence or excess — to then produce the counter effect of becoming aware of a higher and perhaps more definitive consciousness, can be realized through 'The *three doors* of magic' or, *ritual*, *dream* and *ecstasy*.

The Kabbalistic tree illustrated on the opposite page, simplifies this mechanism.

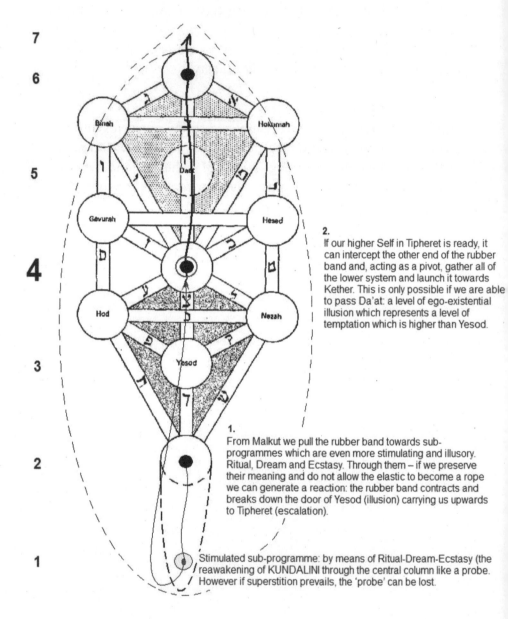

7

6

5

4

3

2

1

2.
If our higher Self in Tipheret is ready, it can intercept the other end of the rubber band and, acting as a pivot, gather all of the lower system and launch it towards Kether. This is only possible if we are able to pass Da'at: a level of ego-existential illusion which represents a level of temptation which is higher than Yesod.

1.
From Malkut we pull the rubber band towards sub-programmes which are even more stimulating and illusory. Ritual, Dream and Ecstasy. Through them – if we preserve their meaning and do not allow the elastic to become a rope we can generate a reaction: the rubber band contracts and breaks down the door of Yesod (illusion) carrying us upwards to Tipheret (escalation).

Stimulated sub-programme: by means of Ritual-Dream-Ecstasy (the reawakening of KUNDALINI through the central column like a probe. However if superstition prevails, the 'probe' can be lost.

We can investigate, fantasize and imagine ritual, dream and ecstasy, using the traditions and practices which are chiefly employed by each 'door', those which have worked leaving one particular aspect to take priority over others, or have been used to open others.

For example all the Western mystery traditions turn to ritual because it is a symbolic-archetypical psycho-drama suitable for activating certain states of consciousness and evoking symbolic correspondences: characters, energies and profound faculties in relation to transcendent planes upon which heroes, gods and hosts of angels can be projected, to satisfy or dominate.

Shamanism however exalts the dimensions of dream to explore the self and unknown faculties and realities, just as the use of psycho-active substances, or meditation, the stimulation of the *Kundalini* and more specifically, mysticism and Tantrism (much closer to each other than you might imagine) explore ecstasy as a door to higher worlds.

The *Endoteric* Path

Thoughts on the Spiritual Search and Teaching

Any pre-modern spirituality that does not come to terms with modernity and post-modernity has no chance of survival in tomorrow's world.

Ken Wilber – The Future of Religion

I would like at this point to share some reflections most of all with spiritual seekers and with those who are involved in teaching and exploring these themes.

Up to now we have outlined the masks of global (self) deceit as well as cognitive and practical perspectives on exploring, living and even proposing concrete directions for achieving greater awareness and perhaps, more mature choices in life.

If from a certain angle our reality appears tragic and inevitable, from another point of view all that has been achieved is in part, just the result of our individual/collective choices. It is the work of artificial conditioning aimed at creating and feeding a way of thinking that forces us inside the strict confines of a circuit of illusions: one that is so convincing that it renders our suggestion of reality totally real and insistent. And when we talk about it and we complain, not without an infantile sense of enthusiasm of presuming that we have understood what others have not, we continue in fact, to feed a catatonic and defeatist line of reality, shock-absorbed by a series of 'venting valves' and palliative satisfactions. Some are particularly banal (football, sexy models, summer holidays and perhaps professional gratification), others are more sophisticated (courses, seminars, New Age and others). All are perfectly delivered to intercept our higher aspirations thanks to their subtle but effective alibis which nevertheless make us feel we are on the right track, pacified and reassured.

The traps of the ego are increasingly sophisticated and yet we know that the human being will never be able to really grow if it does not liberate itself from its obsession with itself, with its own masks, fame and above all its fear of nothingness which, in order to alleviate, it is ready to sell itself for just any old illusion. The darkness of consciousness becomes the light of vanity in any context that offers a framework: health or disease, wealth or poverty, wild ideas or morality, protest or conformism. We are nevertheless kept at a distance from ourselves.

This moment in history seems to be crucial and potentially perfect for *planning a redemption of consciousness*, for preparing us for 'something' that we feel in the air: outside, but above all *inside* ourselves. Disenchanted by all the illusions that are administered to us, we are finally finding enchantment in the one true and authentic reference, the one that in the end we feel and recognize as the real and definitive reference of consciousness: ourselves.
In 1938, Karl Jaspers, a psychologist and philosopher of the last century was already describing a scenario which is similar in many ways to what we are experiencing now. He spoke of the need for a 'philosophy of existence' which would be able to 'take the origin of reality by surprise and grasp it in the same

way as I, through a process of self reflection, in the intimacy of my actions manage to catch myself out '. And then adds: 'Men who had the possibility of being themselves woke up in that pitiless atmosphere which had negated the individuality of the individual personality. They wanted to take themselves seriously; they searched for the reality that was hidden; they wanted to know what was knowable; and they thought that by understanding themselves they could arrive at the origins of their being. But even that movement of thought was often wrapped up in a deceptive net of levelling, transforming itself into a tumultuous and pathetic philosophy of feeling and life. The will to recognize one's own being, perverted into the satisfaction of pure vitality; indigenous will into a craving for primitiveness, a sense of rank into the betrayal of a genuine hierarchy of values'.

National socialism was preparing to set fire to the dust and Jaspers a victim of persecution had to keep quiet. But certainly, like Orwell, he was not mistaken and with history repeating itself, his intuition is still kept alive.

Today the struggle for an authentic understanding of the self is mortified by the same levelling, though no longer inflicted by violence, it is established with more subtle and deadly social and cultural sedatives which, with implacable efficiency, really seem to be leading us to a 'New World Order' without even the pretence of an authentic human renaissance. Instead we have lukewarm, standardized fantasies, New Age style which, bring that same 'old individual confusion' in through the backdoor with a moralistic, dualistic and clerical ring.

Rebirth has to begin with each individual, from the depths of the True Self, and direct itself towards real change. It is still possible. We have to act so that it does not become just the latest fashion, the same old whim. We must not confuse the search for truth with the search for more sophisticated consumer goods and a more sophisticated ego; or *true being* with the need for well-being and 'understanding'.

Everything we are surrounded by was created by us, fed by us, WE ARE US. We also know that the solution, 'the door', is *inside* of us. The door to a true and immediate reality which, is completely different from what we think we perceive and know. And it also includes science, physics, history and all the kaleidoscopic scenic systems of Form, colours and shadows that make up our culture and its customs.

But I will stop there, as we now need to continue the personal and intimate character of this exploration by asking ourselves the following questions:

What style of life?
What concrete choices?
What possible conclusions?
What words and what silence, what actions and what non-action will really take us 'beyond'?
What truth lies behind all the metaphors?
How can we fully live the meaning of our discoveries?

And then... if we want... what teachings, or better still what kind of sharing is possible? What do we know? What have we learnt?...And *therefore*?

How many times have we heard it said that, in being involved in spiritual research, independent information, natural well-being and inner disciplines we are part of a '*niche*'?

Whether one is a free spirit or independent researcher, or puts into practice alternative information, promotes natural health or sustainable development etc, one is easily accused of being part of a 'niche' that is, of belonging to a minority which is not so much original as totally without influence.

We are at the point in which, if you believe in the soul, in Nature or intelligence you are marginalized.

But now it is time to invert such logic. What about those who pollute, are they right?, Those who use drugs, who cure themselves with chemicals, who alter their own body, who corrupt, who brainwash, who waste, who are selfish towards their own kind, animals and plants, those orthodox thinkers and conformists who have been subjected to a conditioning that is passed off as 'values'. If this is the case then roll on the fall of those values!

We, however, want to practice other values: we are searching for our eternal and cosmic soul, we love and respect life in all its forms, we want to regulate our life on the basis of intelligent and harmonious solutions; we do not put profit and convenience first, we do not consider ourselves 'consumers' and we do not accept that entertainment and distractions are enough in life or that superficial information is sufficient.

We are not just voters and 'subjects', guinea pigs or cannon fodder. We give meaning to words such as love, compassion and friendship. We have to reclaim our universal consciousness, the multi-dimensionality of the human being, of every man and woman, our liberty and our profound intelligence: our divine nature. We applaud the dignity of the human being, we search for truth. Well, if this is what it means to be part of the 'niche', so be it. We are in good company. We are the silent majority.

A majority that has to unite its strength, refer to serious and competent information, clarify not only research themes and recent discoveries but themes with a real social impact that are often treated with great superficiality. Let's talk about real well-being, sustainability and avant-garde research, be it scientific or deliciously spiritual, even though such distinctions are fictitious. Clarity is needed on these fundamental themes to avoid profound misunderstandings, sensationalism, manipulation, suggestion and all those placebos aimed at repressing the real reawakening of consciousness; one that requires the presence and the responsibility of everyone.

Taking a look at these themes from the point of view of opposing fronts, we have the Vatican insisting on 'true faith', CICAP (the Italian Commission for the Control of Affirmations on the Paranormal) on 'true science' and the conformist media on 'true life', we already have a new world religion of superficiality, of spiritual ambitiousness, of miracle performing, with its accompanying host of new prophets and saviours.

Certain 'New Age' theories also need to be critically assessed, particularly conspiracy theories when they propose improbable – but fascinating – esoteric-historical reconstructions (most of which were created a couple of centuries ago by the efforts of clever Jesuits fraudsters). We need to re-examine the extra-terrestrial agenda which is not born out by historical, scientific, anthropological and metaphysical accounts; also the proposals of holistic well-being that are often exploited by unscrupulous therapists who damage not only the naive but also serious research, who are then exposed to the mediatic pillory organized by institutional detractors such as the multi-nationals who recruit politicians, professors and managers who are addicted to discrediting dissent: prisoners of the emptiness of their own souls.

We must leave all this pettiness behind, clarify everything and finally enter or better still, determine this New Era of Consciousness, wake up to the illusions, definitively abandon the old dualist paradigms and recover an authentic sense of our humanity and therefore of life.

Humanity's current path invites us to create a future that we can choose for ourselves, founded upon a new scientific, historical and spiritual synthesis.

It is these subjects, or better still with this approach of 'pulling things together' that we particularly need to discuss with researchers and certainly with all those who feel involved in this process of awareness regardless of their experience, education or beliefs. The signs announce times of enormous and rapid change, whether we are ready for them or not.
If from the chaos, a potential for rebirth is also born we can but play in anticipation and ride the waves with will, love and above all courage. Riding the waves means bringing a living message through our own way of being, at home, in the family, the office, factory, school, or university, in the corridors of hospitals and in the bar rather than in art galleries or scientific laboratories.

There is turmoil. All this is turmoil. Let's invite knowledge in with sobriety and purity, with profound honesty and above all with a sincere heart.

The thoughts that have been expressed up till now aim to contribute to an approach that is useful both to a healthy 'search for consciousness' (spirituality, inner search or whatever you want to call it), or 'science', which is nevertheless an indispensible and extremely valid instrument in the exploration of reality.

I certainly believe that these two exploratory fields of science and consciousness have to undoubtedly interact, with reciprocal respect for each others logic and aspire to a definitive (re)integration. We have to allow mysticism and sensitivity to express their perceptions, leave space for spiritual traditions and the timeless knowledge of magic, just as – and rightly so – we need to take account of the enlightened sciences of our time. We need to restore to the sensitivity and individual intuition that is born from the depths of the heart, that trust and those values that have been delegated to the pulpit, cathedrals and dogma for too long and which have taken us away from an authentic taste for things and life.

Existence is complex and made up of forever changing nuances. We need intelligence to stop faith, idealism or sentimentalism degenerating into neuroses and to understand the alchemy of all facets of existence, while maintaining the requisite maturity and forbearance.

It is time to develop further a series of considerations that in the public debate seem to have got caught up in the mesh of rather boring rhetoric.

So far we have established that:

1. It is necessary to be centred
2. To know how to think of others you need to know how to think of yourself
3. It is better to think positively
4. it is better to smile and be optimistic.

Fine. Great.
But now we need to press on and look at the contents. At knowing. At understanding.

Knowledge cannot ignore the need for study even though it goes way beyond mere studying in itself: it is about being disposed towards research and expanding one's consciousness with regard to all aspects of life.

On our own personal path   - which, rather than vaguely describing as 'spiritual' I would prefer to define in a more concrete and all encompassing way as 'existential development' – it is necessary to be aware, or informed. It is also worth saying; conscious, lucid, capable of discernment, critical, and analytical but without ever losing sight of ourselves among the infinite tides of knowledge and current events. In fact knowledgeably making it the reason for clarity and balance, thus conserving a centeredness and forbearance in the definition of ourselves and our intentions.

It is important to know or at least be sufficiently informed about the models of reality that the modern, natural, physical and medical sciences put forward; to know the basics of history, of archaeology and anthropology, just as through a more intelligent and acute capacity we need to inform ourselves with regard to social and political current affairs. We need to be conscious of the context in which to position personal research, the analysis of the self, sentiments, emotions, creativity and in particular our true nature, which is directed towards our real personal existential mission and is much higher in respect to the references of reality and ourselves supplied by our senses and the material world.

With the right approach knowledge leads to wisdom when it does not limit and confuse but supports ethical elaboration, knowledge of the self and a meditation that is able to inspire increasingly authentic values aimed at real well-being. A knowledge of current reality and an awareness of self create become power, an ethical container in which it is possible to achieve an elevated perception of things, events, life and human experience. That is when experience no longer limits itself to just the reality of the material world and a more or less restricted ego but opens up multi-dimensional scenarios of comprehension and life.

Open yourself to knowledge, to becoming aware, to conscious exploration: here are the terms of that practical and holistic existential development for which we are perhaps finally ready, the re-integration of learning with feeling to mature a new human era that is both inevitable and necessary.

This is why the quality of study is so important (obviously it must not be a sterile accumulation of ideas but a motive for understanding, that is well planned and which avails itself of selected and effective references), just as it is necessary to be aware of *current historical* and *geo-political* events – at least the most influential ones – to be knowledgeable about the *spiritual and religious traditions* that have shaped the human history of philosophical, religious and cultural movements and to be up-to-date with the latest developments in science, psychology and medicine. Not forgetting to acquire the information necessary to guide life choices, take care of the physical body, the quality of relationships, one's profession or work and the search for a creative outlet such as cultivating a form of art. It is a call to go beyond inaccuracy, superstition and losing sight of the self and, with the best of intentions, aiming for inner growth and renewal.

We need to commit ourselves to search for the truth of things in this chaos of information and counter-information, half truths and manipulation, science and pseudo-science, existential placebos and fake spirituality.

The evolution of the individual is part of an integrated process of existential development, therefore, to all effects, spiritual. The other part is made up of a knowledge of the self, an emancipation from conditioning, the full realization of our own existence at all levels and the elaboration of a life ethic that enlightens, and renders us spontaneous bearers of truth and light.

The spiritual search is not a vague and transcendental thing but infinitely practical and pragmatic. Anxiety about performance has to be decisively substituted for silence, meditation, openness and profound inner and personal reflection. The spiritual search is not something you can learn in a course or that you prefer to other hobbies. It is not something you have to 'do'. It is also not something simple or within reach. It has something to do with your way of being, feeling and understanding. It is about Living.

It has to do with our entire existence and goes much further than the confines of time, dimensions or biology that seem to define us now. It is much broader – and more demanding – than studying for a degree, pursuing a career, healing your body and mind, being happy or perhaps following the stereotypes of the moment....

The spiritual search has to be your life priority, because it is there that all the other life values come together: if we do not assign it this role, which is what it is for, we are not conducting an authentic search at all.

Work on the spirit is achieved through research that is balanced, not competitive or anxious.

It is fashionable to discuss enlightenment and 'self-realization'. But the truly enlightened person is someone who has achieved it with little, while the unenlightened always has need of something else to achieve it, to feel satisfied, to exist. If there is dissatisfaction it means there is still too much ego. Happiness is achieved through awareness, which is a complete satisfaction of the self.

Awareness is not found in achievement or conquest: it is found in *comprehension*. It does not lie in the possession of something but in the comprehension of everything, without possessing anything. It is Love.

The soul aspires to awareness while the ego aspires to achievement. Perhaps Consciousness is both: if the pointer on the scales moves to far one way or the other we descend into hypocrisy. The anxiety to achieve according to programmes that are inculcated, rather than being our own, is the true illusion. It is hypocrisy. It is non-life. Cultivating false aspirations is an alibi for not waking up and taking responsibility for ourselves. They are masks and convenient sufferings.

The alternative is not to 'do it for yourself' or to 'do it for others': in both cases, if our mission is just growth, be it egoistic or altruistic and fails to reawaken Consciousness, we are still in the circuit of the ego and the mind. It is only when we come out of the ego and stop constantly posing the problem of our enlightenment and happiness, because *we are* and that is enough, that we go *beyond*: we are 'in the world but not of this world'.

'Am I enlightened?', if it is the mind that is asking, then we are in the ego, with the risk that our aspirations are fake and induced. However, if inquietude is the mover of the soul (which

237

does not ask but 'feels'), then we are in the Absolute Being: the soul does not even ask, it acts motivated by its own existence. We are like divers who have passed out in their diving suits...

More often than not spiritual growth is triggered when, conscious of the increasingly obvious, unsupportable and globalized manipulation, we begin to interest ourselves in political dialogue, UFOs, meditation, hidden archaeology and holistic well-being. We take courses and seminars, read books and magazines follow up various indications, methods and perhaps some interesting, liberating and satisfying ideas, very often loosing sight of the path, our original question and the intention and needs that sent us in that particular direction in the first place . We do not realize that the search is first and foremost, a search for meaning.

Then, when we acknowledge the chaos we have ended up in, a certain natural refusal is aroused, a sort of cynicism, or else we go in the opposite direction, into excess becoming prey to one of the many cults or sects in which gurus or novel preachers, as on the threshold of the year one thousand, crawl out of the woodwork waving bibles and gospels for 2012.

Basically we pass from one illusion to another, from one suggestion to another, from one dream to another, one which more often than not transforms into a living nightmare. Well-intentioned references, masters, healers, speakers of all kinds can be valid stimuli: formative points of reference and fonts of inspiration but we must ineludibly drag ourselves away and leave them all behind. And, it will be they themselves – If they are authentic – who will be the first to applaud our decision, our step forward, our liberation from them and their teachings.

What have you learnt? Where is your mastery? Do you want to be a student forever? An eternal course-goer?

Discipline, rules and devotion are the paths to discovering ourselves, for getting closer to our centre, our intelligence and learning to take responsibility. We do not need to believe in eternal schools, unrenounceable references, dogmas and saviours, or a population of enlightened ones. We need to believe in individuals who are free and aware. We need to believe in the people of the world.

Schools, because they are just that, have a limited time span, otherwise they are not schools but sects and cults. It is fine to share a specific project but only on the condition that the project is also yours, one that is persevered with and has time dedicated to it: in fact the realization of your own Personal Project.
But watch out: the wrong means cannot lead to the right ends. Spiritual victory is not measured by having reached the goal but by what you used to get there.

If you do not comprehend that you are Buddha,
What sense is there in looking for wealth outside of yourself?
If you cannot spontaneously meditate
What will you gain by distancing your thoughts?
If you do not know how to harmonize the practice of meditation
with your life,
are you not, probably, just a confused imbecile?
If you do not intuitively acquire the vision of enlightenment,
what use is a systematic search?
If you live thanks to an energy and a time that you do not
belong to,
if you waste your life, who will pay your debts in the future?
Dressed just in cotton rags

what does the ascetic gain by searching for the cold of winter
down here?
The novice who doubles in strength but does not receive a
complete education
is like an ant who tries to climb a mountain of sand:
he does not achieve anything!
Accumulating education without managing to grasp the true
nature of the mind,
Is like dying of hunger in front of an overflowing larder.
[...]
Finally, comprehend, the essence of the teaching in this life,
and practice it!

Ghesce Ciapu

You are accustomed to authority or the atmosphere of authority which you think will lead you to spirituality. You think and hope that another can, by his extraordinary powers – a miracle – transport you to this realm of eternal freedom which is Happiness.

Jiddu Krishnamurti

We can only get to know the criteria that guide us when an overbearing need to create order is born inside of us.

However before pursuing a 'spiritual' life or exploring alternative themes, cultures and esoteric techniques, or even experiences that are more or less esoteric, we need to define our real objective. There is no point in losing ourselves in labels such as 'inner path', 'spiritual search', 'reawakening consciousness' or 'enlightenment' if they lack content. Before we do anything else we have to clarify:

1. What needs we are responding to
2. The role of the personal ego
3. Our mission.

The result is certainly a concrete cosmic broadening of knowledge, of the awareness and consciousness of the Self and of our own role as individuals in the world, as expressions of the All. But in the end, the goal is to be happy in a reality that we render happy, to which we give the truest, broadest and most beautiful meaning possible.

The key to the most authentic happiness is **awareness**, which is true realization, knowledge, wisdom and love. Recovering a sense of faith in ourselves, discovering our talents, recovering a sense of friendship, of a love for Nature. Recovering the meaning of life, but also that of pain and death.

And all of this in everyday life, considering and comprehending all the circumstances in which we find ourselves and for whatever reason are called upon to live. For such realization we can work in a thousand ways, even by renouncing the magic and esoteric because spiritual realization is a real and practical process.

It is enough to have a sense of ethics: of *being* and not of having, of *how* to live of *how* to do things, independent of the contingency of choices. Spirituality is not the automatic fruit of meditation, esotericism or healing magic. Perhaps we are already spiritual and if we like, also a little magic, if we work in an intelligent and constructive way, animated by the will, common sense and sincere love. When we live, work, raise a family, educate children or create better existential conditions for ourselves and the reality we are a part of, we are *creating*

241

for the development of our consciousness whether we are aware of it or not.

Many of us already put this into practice despite all the limits and conditioning supplied by our ailing society. We are spiritual when we are not selfish and egoistical.

From this basis can a different need be triggered? A thirst for greater consciousness and awareness? For a higher 'healing and 'evolution'? For a more comprehensive 'realization'? Certainly.

In general this drive is born out of profound difficulty (shock, trauma, pain, crisis, illness, breakdown...), or from a more subtle and general sense of unease about life for which we search for a cure. It also comes from searching for the answers to the new questions that our life experience gives birth to. From that disquiet the need for some kind of reference is born, perhaps a pathway, even though it is better that everyone always traces their own, original, unique and unrepeatable existential path.

That personal path cannot help but be therapeutic: knowledge of the true Self leads to the healing of our defects and identification. Such defects – according to holistic and traditional disciplines – lie behind all successive diseases and impede the attainment of a healthy life ethic. Being in balance means that we can more easily move aside the limits that restrict us, just as we can also rid ourselves of phantoms from the past. These are the conditions that have to be confronted first before we attempt to explore those that lie deeper and require more effort.

From there a further yearning for discovery can be born, a thirst for knowledge, for a greater consciousness of all that is and of the reality in which we live. We can begin with the ethical duty of achieving happiness and well-being, progressively arriving at a true knowledge consisting of awareness and, perhaps, nostalgia.

We want to 'understand', and in understanding truly 'be'. But the commitment can prove arduous; we need to bear in mind that what we discover along the way might not be easy or pleasant: we could perhaps compare it to taking the 'red pill' in the film Matrix!

We then move from a cultural, ethical or therapeutic drive, to an existential need, or if we prefer, therapeutic in the most radical sense. The search for a deeper meaning is born and therefore an awareness not only of our identity but also a sense of direction and eventually, a sense of the direction of all *human beings*, of our essential 'humanity'.

We enter into a process linked to spirituality as a search for identity and above all as a deep search for wisdom, that inspires the daily choices of life with the values of our own consciousness, one that has been progressively awakened. Nothing could be more concrete and pragmatic!

Through meditation, which transcends therapy by containing it, we enter into a state of communion: into a current that naturally carries us on a path of comprehension, of evolution and, if we allow it to, of happiness. In virtue of the fact that it is being progressively realized, our daily life becomes extraordinary in its simplicity. Through its earthly vicissitudes, though problematic and difficult, a taste for life is rediscovered in its ordinary and intrinsic worth.

We begin to desire a certain syntony with nature and all the expressions of life and begin to understand aspects which at first we had judged hastily or superficially. As a result of this new found harmony we relate in a more active way with the laws and forces of existence inside and outside of ourselves. We accesses new horizons of the Self, or better still of Being and of the possible. We progressively mature the idea of what can only be called 'Magic': or we harmoniously allow the reality around us to tune in with our renewed inner state. Acting through non-action on the real and on the nature of things, moving within ourselves. It is 'power' in a shamanic sense.

It is no longer 'only' a path that aims at a therapeutic, ethical, meditative or mystical search but one that transforms itself into a *magic* or even *sacred* one: We enter into relationship with the 'sacred', that is with the projections of reality as a manifestation of the Absolute, that we intend to rediscover as such, beginning with ourselves.

Therefore it is important to reflect and distinguish between the assertions: 'I want to go and do a course to feel better and resolve my neuroses or become rich and socially successful' and 'I intend to follow a path of Knowledge'.

Distinguish between:

1) Whether you want to remain in a cultural setting and perhaps equip yourself with ready to use techniques (a bit for yourself and a bit to 'help others' and a bit to soothe the afflictions of an ego that is never satisfied — or badly satisfied) or instead...

2) Whether you intend to *explore the Magic sense of Life*.

They are completely different planes and levels of responsibility: on the first, you search to improve your performance; on the second, you are the scenery maker, producer and director.

A Synthesis of my Working Method

Now let's synthesize the parameters of my personal search into a working method.
The spiritual path possible in this special and exceedingly decadent epoch requires:

- Radical authenticity
- Unconditional purity
- Distance from illusions and their deceptions
- Personal energy
- A Love of truth
- Passion and strength of Will

The aim is to achieve with absolute concreteness, a process of definitive and necessary emancipation; a return to true awareness to access a New Gnosis: a revolutionary Mysticism.

The change, the reawakening and the consequent conquest of new evolutionary frontiers begins from the spiritual centre of each individual, therefore from each one of us, from our heart.

We arrive at it through an 'Endoteric' path, one that is defined in my first book.

The Endoteric path proposes an inner search that is autonomous and most of all private. It is based on the following three aspects which are to be considered as perfectly integrated with one another:

1 – *The cultural aspect*

Today, we have the instruments for being informed. It is true that the 'simple' get to heaven but that does not mean the ignorant or the simpletons. Being unaffected, authentic and pure in heart does not contrast with having the right cognitive instruments. We can therefore welcome the kind of learning that exercises and develops the intellectual, philosophical and speculative faculties. Welcome a knowledge of history, the arts and science, just as religious and esoteric history, theories, experiences, prominent figures of current principles and the relative models of reality: Western, Eastern, ancient and modern. Not forgetting that we also need to take account of social, political and economic events.

2 – *The ethical aspect*

Culture and reflection on its contents has to find an 'ethical container', therefore one that is spiritual or even mystical that can be directed in practical terms. Our inner Grail. In this case we are mostly entering into the merit of personal development in terms of awareness, direction and consciousness. Knowledge and the choice of path is an individual task: group work expresses itself – if necessary – in a successive phase, with sharing and discussion. Meditation, being present in oneself, restoring a relationship with the value of the sacred and a coherent style of life, leads to a personal mysticism: a profound discovery and union with the Higher Self, with existential motivations that are truer and more mature. In the system in which I propose this ethical aspect, cultivating an art-form is considered an element of great support.

3 – *The explorative aspect*

This consists of the multi-dimensional development (and ultra-dimensional) of our explorations, beginning with the investigation of the plane of existence that we have been called to live upon, the plane on which we project our inner reality, and progressively expand our sensitivity by accessing higher levels of consciousness. Esotericism, and in this case I do not hesitate to use the term *magic* more specifically, through its representations becomes an instrument for expanding our faculties and consciousness of reality in an active and aware manner, increasingly revealing our divine nature which can then be applied to the material world of life and thought.

 The three aspects of the *Endoteric Path* have to be integrated in a balanced way: Theory and practice on the self, reality and their potential for expansion. There is no progression of contents but work begins immediately on all aspects, which, taken up again and again slowly evolve to higher (and more profound) levels.

Know the truth of the past,
consciously live the present,
determine the future with trust:
this is what each of us must do
for ourselves and for the free evolution
of Human Consciousness.

This is the opening phrase of the web site of the *Ascension 93 Study Centre* in which it is possible to share your own working reality. As a result of this interaction it is possible to focus on elements and information that access a path of healing, one that I would define as spiritual, consequently, a path towards a more complete:

- Knowledge of the Self
- Consciousness of reality
- Awareness of one's own evolutionary direction

The path to reawakening consciousness cannot but pass through radical commitment and coherent choices in life, to the teaching of absolute liberty and individual responsibility.

The references, methods and techniques proposed today are many, some are authentic, others more superficial, just as the motivations and approaches we choose or are induced to. With the 'Endoteric' path, which consists of readings, practices, meetings and study groups, a profound re-think is proposed on all fronts, on the basis of what is the most interesting, valid and significant. Each person then regulates and applies it with determination to their own personal search.

As the source of personal experimentation is by nature esoteric and highly complex, it would be reductive to limit it to contents and dynamics to a psychological-therapeutic level or to that of dialectic discussion: aspects that nevertheless constitute a spontaneous component of the holistic process and its cultural and spiritual objectives.

The theoretical knowledge is related to a much broader and more mature framework of motivations. The logic and practices proposed are brought together on a plane of sensitivity which is 'other', perhaps a 'true sensitivity, one that eludes conventional filters. Such relationships have to express themselves above all, through the path of silence rather than the word, through meditation rather than speculation, through the energy of the body rather than the energy of the mind.

The working practices that I apply and teach are as follows:

- Meditation as a technique
- Exercise of the body
- Meditation as an expression and way of being
- Breath and the channelling of Prana
- Self-observation and memory of the self
- Consciousness of spiritual parts and soul components
- Emotions as instruments for perceiving reality and the self
- A magic and synchronic vision of reality
- Order and regulation in life and thought
- Use of a diary as an instrument of reviewing and planning
- The refining of a higher sensitivity
- A path of study and research by means of selected references, texts, or even pilgrimages, retreats and specific cultural and social initiatives.

There is a further aspect to consider.

Having decided to follow a spiritual teaching, many delude themselves that all their problems will be resolved straight away and that they will be able to live a peaceful and serene life. Eh no, it is not that easy. To resolve problems it is necessary to impose precise inner work, a programme to achieve and that requires time. But by beginning the instant you have fixed the task to be performed, even though you may not achieve it all, at least leaves an impression. Its mark remains somewhere and the forces of the subconscious begin to circulate through the channel you have dug out. If, however, you do not register anything deeply in your psyche all your existence will pass you by without you ever having been able to achieve anything. When it rains, the water precisely follows the channels that have been dug out. You therefore have to prepare the terrain, you have to prepare the channels so that new life can circulate inside of you.

O.M. Aïvanhov

Personal commitment is needed to render any course profitable, concrete and linear in its unfolding, by studying and applying oneself assiduously. On a *path of consciousness*, commitment has to be proportional to motivation and most of all, to the aspirations declared, that is, to the result that we wish to obtain.

We know that the amount of time and energy at our disposal can be limited, considering the rhythms and needs of daily routines, even though they may contribute to our growth through their *karmic* implications or through other aspects.

We need to not only understand the level of commitment and priority that we want to dedicate to our path but we also need to realistically establish or own objectives (always in continuous evolution) in relation to ourselves and in proportion to the circumstances, time and energy at our disposal. Likewise we need to be realistic about that of that any eventual 'facilitator' (I purposely do not want to speak of gurus or masters, but travel companions who help each other on the basis of who has the greatest competence and experience) who should respond honestly when declaring whether or not a certain result can be achieved and on what terms: whether it is right to offer it now or to wait because of particular circumstances.

That result has to be attainable in its authenticity and truthfulness and not through illusory results that clever 'communicators' may have devised to sell their own inefficiency. People should aspire to objectives that can be reached, ones that are real, concrete and measurable on a level of personal growth that is applied to the reality of things. Only if we accept and comprehend our respective limits can we continue to evolve, by respecting what they currently consist of and how they function.

On the one hand, the person has to be helped to establish objectives which are in line with the level of commitment declared or the time/energy they actually have available and on the other, those who 'facilitate' have to decide to accept the requested task with honesty, for the good of the person without forcing them, making false promises, or intending to gratifying high and sublime objectives by playing on suggestion and fascination. Such elements, however, often become sufficient or even false objectives for such people, who use them in that guise, to justify themselves with a false goal instead of making a real effort to achieve results. But putting ourselves on the line costs energy and pride: it is sometimes easier to defend our limits and pressing needs with a drawn sword and say what we want to hear rather than open up and question ourselves.

Such conditions do not lead to profitably accessing the field of multi-dimensional, magic explorations of the self and reality: we would be better off remaining within our limits or casually finding a suitable therapeutic path and not pretend to 'Search for The Grail' if we are that badly equipped.

In such cases, it is also necessary to *educate our pretensions* and understand that there is a strict relationship between

251

aspiration and commitment, desire and circumstance, just as there is a difference between an honest promise and a fraudulent one, real satisfaction and illusory gratification.

As in cycling, we must never think about winning the race, just completing the next stage. Or rather, the objective, once reduced to more realistic dimensions, is refined with far-sightedness, expanding towards extraordinary aspirations that in the end, become realistic and legitimate.

However, the meaning of esotericism is not consumed by this: esotericism is not a theoretical and mental teaching, therefore it cannot be sequential or follow any particular logic. All traditions and tales of the Masters remind us that esoteric teaching may follow many different kinds of logic at the same time or perhaps none that we are able to recognize.
But our soul certainly can.

Naturally on a shared path, or one that includes moments of collective discussion we have to be aware of the different levels of the people involved. The advantage of the esoteric approach is that it communicates with everyone: Its message reaches all levels in proportion to motivation and commitment.

In the table on the following page you will find a programme of study and experiences illustrated, that I share in the context of the 'study and meditation groups' that have spontaneously formed as a result of my talks in various Italian cities. These groups – which are open to everyone and free – are an opportunity for in-depth research, following a programme of study and practice which can be done individually and collectively. It is a path which, once having furnished an initial outline, then opens up and develops new themes thanks to other speakers and researchers, creating a self-managed process on the basis of a series of projects and a timetable chosen together.

Every individual studies and works on a personal level to then, in the context of the group, discuss and compare with others, broadening their opportunities for knowledge and also contributing to cultural initiatives that create further occasions for sharing information and culture.

Group meetings are periodically organized to assess what point has been reached in the learning process, to examine on-going research, respond to questions and supply additional stimuli based on the characteristics of each group.

In the following working table the path is developed 'progressively' because in the West we are inclined to describe the process of re-awakening and the evolution of Consciousness as a kind of progressive edification, of a path, or a sequence of actions that allow us to reawaken to ourselves and comprehend reality.

The West is more inclined towards the idea of exploration, of conquest, whereas in the East there is more of a propensity to use the idea of taking away: there is nothing to construct, to conquer: in fact we need to 'remove the dust from the mirror', remove the overlays that stop us from really being ourselves. For the East, we are talking about demolishing the filters of conformism and false knowledge.

Suggested Practices and Tasks

Study and Meditation	BODY	**Intent**	Silence
Integrated Inner Harmonizing			
Perception (focused on body and senses)			
5+1 Tibetan Rites	SENSES		Order
Focus and Presence		**Self-observation**	
Breathing techniques			
Self-Observation			
Self-Remembering	EMOTIONS		Mapping
Mapping of the personalities			
Emotions as senses		'Centre of Mass'	
Recapitulation & Goal-Setting			
New Sensitivity	FACULTIES		Integration
Synchronic and Magic view of Life		**Love**	
Understanding			Reconnection
Moving the 'Assemblage Point'			
		Will	Enlightenment

Death-Rebirth
Metamorphosis

RE-EVOLVED
CONSCIOUSNESS

In reality both Traditions, that of the West just as that of the East, aim to reawaken Consciousness and an evolution of the self through human experience that is active and aware. However, in their esoteric guise – or as the relationship between one and the other superficially appears - they overshadow one another. The East indicates a reawakening to the self as reaching the goal, the contemplation of the real Self, the *diver* finally reawakened in his diving suit, but we are 'only' talking about recovering from a handicap: of being aware of what we really are and not of an evolutionary phenomenon in itself. On the other hand it would seem that the West, in its explorative craving, avoids exploring reality through Consciousness and limits itself to exploring only with the mind: the diver continues to sleep and pretends that his suit is the active subject of real exploration. It seems that, Easterners arrive at Consciousness and enjoy it passively, without remembering that it is their evolutionary mission and Westerners explore their false identity with the mind, exclusively evolving in the illusion in which they are immersed.

In their esoteric essence, Eastern and Western Traditions certainly do not fall into this trap, but often seem to lack discernment between the means and the ends as regards the interpretation of teachings and techniques, as well as a complete vision of the entirety of the process that relates to our growing consciousness.

Some of the techniques used in study groups will be made available on the Web or editorially to encourage individual work.

A Mistake to be Avoided

The only way to be wise is to not understand everything.

Thomas Moore

We have to leave room for mystery and accept the gaps in our knowledge that leave us a precious margin of imponderability because this is the real mover of evolution.

Nicola Cusano (1401-1464), Theologist, Vatican Ambassador, as well as Philosopher, Astronomer and Mathematician of German origin, along with Shunruy Suzuki (1904-1971), the famous Zen Master, both spoke of a 'holy ignorance' as the essence of wisdom.

American author Thomas Moore in *The Soul's Religion* makes a recommendation:
'Spiritual intelligence requires a particular kind of emptiness, a sophisticated ignorance, an increasing ability to forget what you know and give up the need to understand.[...] Free from the pretence of knowledge we can go deeper, pose more pertinent questions and be transformed as people rather than limiting ourselves to stimulating the mind.'
This search for a mystic participation in life goes beyond the materialistic (and neurotic) teaching of the knowledge. Attention though, the mind and reason are not to be excluded. As Moore himself states: "The central paradox, of course, is that it takes considerable knowledge and thoughtfulness to arrive at Nicolas of Cusa's *educated ignorance*". Certainly it is only right and proper to investigate, explore, know and understand, nevertheless it is necessary to leave space for the

imponderable, for mystery and the void: Our level of anxiety lowers and, emancipated from the illusion of certainty, we can freely explore the mysteries of existence.

A respect for the sense of mystery goes arm in arm with abstaining from hasty judgment, drawing conclusions and sometimes even from talking. The God that can be thought of is not the ultimate God, just as the truth revealed is no longer the Truth.

Epilogue

If you lack a spiritual vision, life is gloomy, sad, difficult and therefore in vain.

From my Diary – 2010

During conferences and meetings, I have noticed that, just as for some it is enough to read a few books, attend a conference from time to time or venture on certain experiential seminars, others want a more structured and continuative path, to explore concepts and practices in more depth.
Some wish to continue a more involved search at an individual or group level, others again, dream of living a different life. And it is this theme that I would like to explore with you now.

In effect, with complete respect for responsibility and self-determination and absolute individual freedom in the 'search' for one's own Path and the full realization of one's own personal story, whether it be for those who have no other pretences (because this 'search' is in itself grandiose and extraordinary!), or, and most of all, for those who intend to apply the reflections of a new awareness to their own daily lives; we have to use instruments that are more articulate and operational than books, discussions or methods of growth, even though they are stimulating, innovative and significant as such.

Leaving aside what each person wishes and feels they want to do, in complete freedom, autonomy and consciousness, an 'outlet' is needed that is stimulating fun and concrete. Collective maturation leads to the need for a shared project that can be achieved with great passion and enthusiasm, to a desire to create something concrete that is both beautiful and different.

That's fine ... let's do it.

For example, the idea of creating meeting points and thought workshops is valid if they allow for continued experiences and study programmes as part of shared projects in a broader sense. In this way free and independent research is promoted which helps to provide us with the instruments needed for learning. Being aware of the cause, we can grow and be self-determined, reawakening to an inner awareness that is more authentic and innovative. A total plan has more impact than the occasional conference, a seminar or casual meeting and makes room for a more in-depth multi-disciplinary approach just as continuity is more efficient at building on the level of personal growth.

It is fine to want to create and share healthy opportunities that are new and stimulating but the individual is and must always remain at the centre: the responsible protagonist, master and healer of his/herself, a humble and intelligent apprentice, a free and self-determined researcher: the only and ultimate judge of his/herself.

I believe in a *new personal order.*

We need to re-enter ourselves to create the conditions for a radical reawakening of human and natural values. We need to be aware and exit from our mental torpor. To look around us and be truly indignant, so much so that we really have the courage to 'change'.

Radical global changes, perhaps drastic and willy–nilly are what awaits us, whether it be in one year or two hundred. And we do not need to be grand economists, sociologists or rocket scientists to see it coming.

Nature is really the basic reference that needs to be restored, not only as an expression of the living planet through which we can rediscover our lost alliance but as a concept, as an *existential place* to rediscover ourselves, the value of life and a sense of reality. The place to correct the path of a failing story and find the key to possible evolution.

The relationship with nature cannot be restored through rituals, evocations, formulas or occasional moments of consciousness, which are full of sentimentalism rather than real awareness. That is only an abstract approach.
A magic and sacred relationship with nature is only restored when one consciously begins to dig the ground and create a vegetable garden.

We have to begin with ourselves: by returning to the most elementary and basic essentials of *what we are*. So that each one of us can finally draw on the inner motivation linked to our *own* awareness and learn to be masters of ourselves and our own dreams.

Appendix I

The Fundamental Functions of the Universe of Form

niversal Functions	Sephiroth	Chakra	Emotions		Faculties	Mantra	Attitude	Buddhism	Ashtanga Yoga
			Positive	Negative					
Frequency	Malkuth	coccyx	happiness	unhappiness	dimensions/aura	A	action	right action	Yama
Interaction	Yesod	genitals	security	insecurity	memory	E1	continuity-coherence	right mindfulness	Nyama
acred Geometry	Hod/Netzach	plexus	joy	suffering	mind	E2	depth	right concentration	Asana
anent Consciousness	Tipheret	heart	love	hate	intent	O1	welcome-availability	right intention	Pranayama
Correspondence	Geburah/Chesed	throat	gaiety	sadness	para-telepathy	O2	exploration-movement	right effort	Pratyahara
Synchronicity	Daath	"mobile"	completeness	defeat	emotions	IAOUE-EUOAI	art-creativity	right speech	Dharana
Chaos	Binah/Chockmah	3rd eye	serenity	restlessness	dream	U	renovation-adaptability	right livelihood	Dyana
Complexity	Kether	crown	beatitude	anguish	consciousness	I	sharing-generation	right view	Samadhi

Frequency

All things have their own 'frequency', an existential code that establishes their working and evolutionary programme at every scale. This code is formed by a univocal and specific combination of the eight fundamental functions that caused the manifestation of the object: be it simple or complex, inanimate or living. As dowsers well know, identical frequencies do not exist: each Form has its own *frequency* and rhythm making it compatible with and distinguishing it from other Form that share its plane of reality (dimensional frequency).

The Primordial Consciousness, in its creative functions, runs, defines, places and distinguishes in zero time – or at infinite speed - every line of reality and every single Form manifest inside universes: renewing in each manifestation the primordial meeting of the laws, continually and contemporaneously, which manifest in every part, the All.

261

We can also imagine it like this: Consciousness, is a kind of 'immovable mover', it works to vibrate and irradiate *planes of existence*. The vibration and sound are concepts and *forces* that assume a truly essential significance.

The previous function can also be represented by the metaphysical and archetypical atoms that were already being thought of in the IV century a.C. by Democritus and were later perfected by the philosopher Leibniz, father of the infinitesimal calculus and precursor to fractal mathematics. In the seventeen hundreds he introduced the *Theory of Monads*, which describes infinitesimal particles multiplied all over the universe which contain all things within themselves.

Monads only exist in the present, they are everywhere at any given moment, or they possess inside themselves all places and all times.

According to our point of view we can therefore talk about omnipresent monads, in practice a 'sole atom' (reviving the jargon of Democritus) that runs infinitely through the universe bringing to all things the information necessary for their creation (the universal laws combined in a vibratory code), or even the same 'One' as an archetypical matrix that is immobile and pulsating and which issues and creates space-time planes of existence as sounds and rippling waves – for us, they are the world we live in – the infinite hologram. The example fits with that of *strings* – which like the chords of a guitar – by vibrating and creating interference between themselves create fields of existence, worlds, as if they were musical chords. Today, in effect, Physics also tends to theorize the existence of just one universal chord, which could perhaps precisely correspond to the *derivative laws* that we are examining here.

262

Interaction

Planes of reality are fields for gathering together *particles of possibility* or potential events.

An event is 'possible' if it is contained within the confines of the laws, in the *world of ideas*. By 'event' we mean any manifestation in the world of Form. Events constitute a potential. But this does not mean that the potential will necessarily be used (manifested, 'happen').

Therefore we have:

- Events which, upon 'arriving' in the universe are used (saturated events, expressed
  as Form or that we read as historical)
- Events that remain unused (unsaturated events, not translated into manifestation and excluded from the choices made by sentient Form).

Saturated events are saturated however on the basis of a determined level of complexity:

1. According to the average range of the *time packet* they belong to
2. In proportion to the being that perceives, determines and uses them.

Consequently they always have a margin of possible saturation (or re-saturation) at a higher level of complexity.

Unsaturated events are not wasted, instead:

- They are re-cycled in other dimensions

- Remain as potentials in our quantum dimensional field (line of reality)
- Develop temporary parallel realities, called 'Echo Worlds'[51]
- In certain conditions with the passage of time they concentrate in particular places, defined as *Temporal Mines*, which are considered magic or sacred.

All Form (atoms, objects, bodies), are already events as such. For this reason they are never 'neutral' as they would be if they were in their primeval state, given that the moment they enter our universe they are oriented towards becoming something coherent and circumscribed within the limits of this specific universal field.

We are talking about a derivative law. In fact, as 'sub-species' of primeval laws, these 'events' will not have a pre-ordained manifestation but are ready to back up whatever arises in any field of successive laws.

In our case events cannot but manifest themselves as Form, being as ours is the *Universe of Form*. However simply speaking of events as Form is reductive because the word 'event' for us is linked to the concept of historical succession, of action, of happening. In effect, defining 'what is an event' depends on who is considering the subject: for a simple stone the event is the stone itself, but for us? And for an even higher being?

As we slowly arrive at more complex and sentient living Form, the concept of event expands and does not only refer to Form as such but also to the variables that influence it or originate it,

---

[51] See also the most recent theories on *Reality Transurfing* by Vadim Zeland and Tom Kenyon's *The Art of Jumping Time Lines*, available online: http://tomkenyon.com/jumping-time-lines.

or the relationship between things interpreted by our mental patterns: the interaction. A more complex Form, for example a multi-dimensional being, will have an even more expanded concept of the events that are the subject of its level of 'attention'.

The psycho-beings that make up our subtle and spiritual eco-system confer a certain *direction* on events, orienting them to safeguard a certain equilibrium or constitute the 'nourishment' they need to maintain themselves and grow.

This orientation is a sign, a valence, that characterizes the event before it 'touches' Form. Before manifesting, every event passes through various levels of orientation corresponding to the various possible intelligences of different orders and grades that are encountered and travelled through. The last of these *territorial entities* is the human being who, by exercising free will and the ability to act on reality, can use the event, that is 'saturate' it, at a given level of complexity and render it *manifest* on its plane of existence.

The *rain* of events – as shamans describe it – is not uniform and regular but follows precise lines of major intensity: for example the *Synchronic Lines*[52] or individual *force lines*.

Near to nodes of the Synchronic Lines it is probable that *Mines of Events* will be found, just as inside of us, near to our inner synchronic nodes we have the *chakra*.

---

[52] The Synchronic Lines (that the ancient Chinese called the 'Back of the Dragon') make up an irregular grid of subtle and spiritual energy streams that envelop the planet at different depths or altitudes (they rarely appear on the Earth's surface). While the more famous 'Leylines' – magnetic/telluric lines – are typically terrestrial, the Synchronic Lines connect the living system of our planet to the Sun and from there to all the living systems of our universe and probably even beyond.

These sites   – outside and inside of us – are particularly important as far as the possibility of exploring dimensions and space-time is concerned.

At the moment given our lack of consciousness, therefore 'inconsistence' on the plane of the real, we are subjected to events rather than being their directors.
We fluctuate chaotically between casual lines of reality, unable to imprint a coherent presence in any of them: analogous to attempting to write in a notebook, but the pen throws itself down and shows up casually between different sheets of paper. It would not be possible to read anything on any of the pages.
If the soul does not 'read', or does not manage to relate to a system of shared values, it is lost. In the absence of values the mind finds refuge in the guise of character and in a simulation of the real, such as our present illusion.

Outside there is nothing but a tangled mass of frequencies and fields of energy and information. An infinite sea of consciousness from which we select, with our current physical senses, just a tiny range of perceptions which, processed by our brain create the collective hologram. And, not only in terms of the reality of the senses but most of all as a reality adapted to our *belief systems*, which is then programmed by those who want to force us into an oblivion of ourselves inside the *matrix*, censuring our access to reality both collectively and individually.

Only through the expansion of consciousness can we overcome our shortcomings and conditioning and defeat those 'dominators' that we ourselves continually nourish. This is the real challenge, not that of resisting or entering into senseless conflicts, which in fact feeds the behaviour pattern that we have allowed to inculcate us and that we avoid analyzing and removing. Behaviour which continues to feed our mental programmes and sense perception and makes us identify with such programmes.

Today we are not creators. We are consumers who casually dissipate energy on the achievement and application of illusions and programmes that do not belong to us. And so the mind and body progressively degenerate: we consume, eat, sleep, and run around our wheels like hamsters; things that would be unnecessary if we truly lived our level of existence and interacted with what is real.

Sacred Geometry

This function defines the multi-dimensional-holographic grid within which all Form 'gathers mass'. It defines the *coordinates,* where all Form can manifest itself with regard to a field of perception on the basis of precise relationships which lie 'upstream' in respect to our normal cerebral processes.

It is a basic geometry which repeats itself in the macrocosm as in the microcosm: a 'sacred geometry' that by correspondence connects all points of the universe and time, in the great as in the small. When that geometry is reproduced in all its possible patterns it is able to call up cosmic energies and allows us to move from one point in time and space to another, on physical, astral, mental and spiritual levels. This is why there was a need to reproduce it in Ancient Temples, in Cathedrals, on Talismans, Mandala, in the form of Magic Ceremonies, in Seals, in Yoga positions and Sacred Dance. It is reproduced in our mind, in our DNA in its totality, just as in our subtle bodies (the Merkaba) to activate our latent faculties and – it releases us from the limits that constrain us inside a pre-selected programme of reality -

allowing us to travel in time, space and between the dimensions of the possible.

In practice, sacred geometry is that *archetypical geometry* that defines the map of dimensional and space-time territory within which every Form positions itself in perfect dynamic juxtaposition with everything else.
Archetypical geometries, which recur on all scales of manifestation, are the basis of all the spatial and inter-dimensional correspondences between things, events and living beings.

For this reason sacred geometry establishes the weight, measure and relationship between all things, 'as above so below'. Closely connected to *frequency* (remember that all laws function according to one another) it presides over the formation of our subtle bodies (affecting the physical body), just as our DNA, in relation to the dimensions and our reference levels of consciousness.

Immanent Consciousness

This is the function on the basis of which an 'organized awareness', or a divine principle, can move around inside a universe and, in our case, in the worlds and manifestations of Form. This *divine principle*, as law, is present in every Form and adapts itself, or we can say activates itself and potentially makes itself manifest on the basis of the complexity of the Form in which it participates, or better still 'uses' as an experiential vehicle.

It is a 'fragment of the mirror', more or less aware and sentient: from a mere passive drowsy presence to a reawakened and working divine spark.

It is a principle of spiritual identity which is nevertheless present in every Form and able to reflect the All. This law leads to Cosmic Consciousness in Form, in every single Form of the Universe (principle of immanence).

In complex Form this 'presence' develops so that it can actively participate in universal dynamics, to sustain and even consciously guide the entire evolutionary cosmic experience.

Correspondence

Every variation and transformation regarding any Form (for example, from mass to energy and vice versa) has its rightful compensation somewhere, in other mass and energy, so that total equilibrium can be maintained.

This does not mean that for every transformation, in every Form instant to instant the compensation has to uniformly involve the entire universe. It only involves those systems, those Form, that are in someway linked or 'correspond' – even over space-time distance – with the acting Form, by means of a kind of *entanglement*[53] , that we will now explore in a metaphysical sense.

---

[53] The phenomenon of *entanglement* is a quantum phenomenon in which the quantum state of two objects is seen as strictly dependent on one another, even though the objects are spatially separated. The phenomenon described is a little bizarre it must be said, so much so that Einstein himself, labeled it as a sinister action at a distance and considered all quantum theory 'incomplete' in that it lead to non-localized phenomena.

Here is one of the basic principles of Hermeticism: 'similar responds to similar'. But what does being *similar* mean? It does not mean that two Forms look alike or necessarily have the same origin, and not even that they participate in the same space-time territory which would connect them to relationships of cause and effect.

Instead, the similarity is based upon a relationship of temporal or perhaps we should say *evolutionary*, concordance. One Form may correspond to another because it is close as regards its position inside the cone of complexity. Basically, the Form interact because they have similar evolutionary speeds or levels of complexity (or a speed towards complexity) which are comparable. Their evolutionary level is set down on a plane of correspondence regardless of the distance between them or any other kind of relationship.

Time (the 'evolutionary tension') is an alchemical parameter for each Form. It is the measure of the transformation of Form inside of a flow of complexity. Form with different origins, even though they may be at a distance from one another in space-time, are 'similar' if they have a similar evolutionary drive. In effect they are 'close' to one another in the evolutionary cone and their 'nodes of complexity' are comparable.

The laws of Correspondence therefore measure the 'evolutionary tension' of all Form, providing the necessary correspondences to maintain balance in the system in general.

Entanglement is at the basis of emerging technologies of quantum computers and of quantum cryptography and recent experiments relative to so called quantum tele-transport. It makes one think that entanglement could prove to be a very important factor in this Universe (extract from the article by Renato Pagliaro entitled, 'The Roots of Entanglement', source www.scienzaeconoscenza.it).

All of this works outside of our awareness: our current perceptions exclude or attribute these relationships to much more restrained and apparent phenomenon that we call 'cause and effect', which is justified by our mental processes.

Correspondence is the 'law of attraction' that puts into selective relationship all Form and the events between them: it is the true connection, the network and the communication criteria of the global *system-matrix*.

Correspondence not only functions on an energetic level, let's say physical, but also on a mental level, in the issue of thoughts, events and actions, outside of space-time but also inter-dimensionally.

It is the origin of telepathy, the power of synchronicity rather than contactism or the communication between different entities or those belonging to different levels of reality. It occurs as a result of triggering the correspondence on the plane of evolutionary syntony, just as the frequencies (derivative laws described earlier) connect Form on a level of vibrational syntony.

Synchronicity

Synchronicity organizes events – let's say that it optimizes their interaction – as part of the evolution of the system regardless of whether we are aware of it or not.
'Synchronicity' was the term used by psychologist Carl Gustav Jung to describe the alignment of universal forces with the life experience of the individual.

271

Jung believed that some (if not all) coincidences do not just happen merely by chance, but that they are literally 'co-incidents', or the alignment of universal forces that create precise events and circumstances. The process for becoming intuitively aware and acting in harmony with these forces is what Jung meant by the term 'individuation'. Jung said that individuation allows a person to understand surrounding events as a result of the communication between their individual state of consciousness and the collective unconscious.

From a magic point of view it means comprehending the criteria through which synchronicity operates: it is interesting to note that once having acquired a new awareness, – that is once having overcome the needs of the illusory ego – the Will no longer expresses itself by intervening in synchronicity, given that it knows how to intuit the absolute harmony of universal motivations.

On a spiritual level the same concept of 'synchronic intervention' – a power that is often sought after as an instrument for influencing events – makes no sense. On a magic level it is technically very complicated and dangerous, given the impossibility of managing with absolute precision all the necessary compensation needed to balance out any interference. It is a vain pretence, even though we may want to achieve it in order to help others and it is even more dangerous if personal advantage is brought into play. However, we have to set it apart from a simple and spontaneous offer of directed thought, perhaps in a moment of prayer, meditation or taking stock, actions which do not implicate a manipulation of reality or the nature of things but are found in the higher dimension of love. Synchronic intervention can be obtained with the intercession of higher forces, which are endowed with a much higher vision (but not absolute!) and therefore, by delegating the compensatory mechanism. But, these same forces will make us pay a high price for their services. There is another way in which it is possible to achieve this power in a more harmonious manner: if one were the *Absolute Consciousness and Indifferent* but if that were the case one would not want to intervene in anything.

Understanding the criteria of synchronicity also means being able to carry out temporal prospecting (so-called forecasts or divinations) regardless of method or whether or how much it is coded (Tarot, I-Ching, geomancy etc.) or whether it is an intercession on the part of mediating forces (the Oracle). In fact, by entering into direct syntony with synchronicity, with every event and with every thing we would be able to know about all events and all things (shamans talk about life as a 'divination table').

Jung spoke of synchronicity as an 'a-causal principle of connection', in other words a pattern of connections that function outside of causality.

From a magic-esoteric point of view, by means of synchronicity it is possible to interact with events outside of time and the laws of cause and effect, the recalling of which, thanks to the *laws of attraction*, achieves precise effects and results 'here and now', directly and immediately; leaving *external intention* working, as Vadim Zeland describes[54].

In fact, synchronicity is the cosmic law that selects events and makes them available – withdrawing them from the 'universal mind' – as part of the natural evolution and conservation of the system-universe, obviously over and above our current comprehension of its mechanisms.

---

[54] ZELAND Vadim - *A Rustle of Morning Stars*, 2008.

From a certain point of view, synchronicity could explain certain para-psychological phenomena or so called 'miracles'. Phenomena that elude simple causes because we do not know how to read the mechanisms of nature on a wider scale and we exclude all of the possibilities that could be (if we want) effectively achieved. For this reason I generally consider the use of the term 'paranormal' imprecise. Although it may elude us, there is always a cause: it can be found on other planes or be positioned somewhere else in time, even ahead, but it is always there. While the laws of correspondence work on immediate interactions (correspondences to be precise), synchronicity operates in the dynamics of cause and effect, even though it is spread out over all universal dimensions and consequently imperceptible in cases where its own sensitivity is not likewise dilated.

The comprehension of this universal law coincides with a major understanding of reality beyond the appearances of cause and effect. It means tuning in beyond the *local mind*.
Understanding synchronicity can also be useful, for example in the investigation of telekinetic phenomena. No actual force is used to 'move' an object, rather it simply calls up from the reservoir of all possible events, the circumstances in which the object is displayed in a different way. That is valid for objects but also for events and *lines of life*, without the restrictions of space, time or dimensions and beyond all limits and conditions.

It is also important to remember that while Alchemy and 'Esoteric Physics' aim to investigate reality and obtain particular effects by means of a profound understanding of the laws and mechanisms that govern it, Magic, completely regardless of any knowledge of causes, mechanisms or 'laws' – the 'science of the sciences' – pursues the immediate and unconditioned achievement of the desired effect. One that is synchronically called up from the dimension of the possible, whatever it is, without any intermediate passages, exercise of force or intervention 'from inside' of its own line of reality.

The 'thing' happens and that is enough. Magic has nothing to do with laws and processes: it is the absolute power of manifestation. Magic is allowing reality to assume the shape of its own will: a will that is total, complete and integral. Because it is so powerful it can call up – from the sea of infinite possibilities of existence – the necessary circumstances for the unconditional realization of any intent that is desired.

Chaos

Chaos is always the successive order. We intuit it as a combination of dimensions without substance, of non-directed virtual events, that are not oriented in time and unintelligible, conserved indistinctly and casually in the field of the possible. We are talking about a very relative concept: beyond the abyss that separates us from the Real, Chaos is the most perfect of orders.

In our growth, however, we can say that chaos represents the successive order. Given that it is a law, our universe is infinitely dynamic because chaos is its constitutive element: this means that there will always be a margin for evolution, an opportunity for optimization, an order of a higher rank that is not yet identified, therefore, there will always be a margin of chaos to 'put in order'. Without chaos we would not be in our universe: it is one of its laws. The universe, however, does not need to be 'resolved' but rather elaborated and *infinitely* lived.

This is really the law that permits evolution, because it renders endlessly fluid the order reached (to then effect a higher order, or at least a different one).

An evolutionary drive is always based on the capacity to call into question an equilibrium, to achieve a new one: our own universe is the result of an anomalous wave: an a-symmetry.

The element of chaos synchronically leads to transformation, in virtue of different and potentially much broader perspectives. Chaos, therefore, is the evolutionary element par excellence from a physical and metaphysical point of view. Through chaos continuous change and transformation is achieved, the demolition of the principles 'fixed and immutable' and the attainment of new 'levels of justice'.

From our point of view, it is the subjective and limited perception of a higher order that we do not know how to interpret, whose dynamics escape our control and understanding.

The physics of chaos is one of the most fascinating frontiers of science. The term 'Chaos Theory' has struck the collective imagination and entered popular culture along with the 'Butterfly Effect': it is said that the slightest flap of a butterfly's wings is able to provoke a hurricane in another part of the world. We are talking about an idiom which contains the mostly technical notion of *sensitive dependence on initial conditions* which is present precisely in Chaos Theory. The idea is that tiny variations in initial conditions produce grand variations in the long term behaviour of a system. Also of interest, the same research applied in the financial field which seeks to interpret and forecast the trends of the global financial markets.

Chaos being a constitutional law, the universe of Form cannot be 'resolved' in a single definitive truth but is continuously 'processed' inclining towards orders that are forever new. Absolute truths or definitive formulas do not exist, but different levels of intelligence applied to processing revised solutions in contexts that are forever new, instant after instant.

More than the truth, we are here to conquer intelligence: the 'ninth law'.

The Arrow of Complexity

The universe to exist has to make its way back in a conscious form to the Absolute Being, therefore 'transcend itself' by means of its existential, living, mental and spiritual dynamics, otherwise, being an *anomaly*, it cannot hold out and is absorbed into the totality: in practice it never existed. However, we are here: which means that – in some way – it works.
The meeting of the basic laws that govern our universe is sustainable if the functionality derived from it produces a superior result, an *added value*, which connects that field of the possible (relative, temporal and material) to the Absolute.

The 'arrow of complexity' indicates the direction needed to produce 'added value'. It is not merely a 'mechanistic' process because it is on the plane of the existential meanings, psychic experience and emotions which develop the evolutionary project: this is why we show the arrow of time simply as 'ideal', given that it is not certain that evolution is so linear (future = evolution) most of all because of the presence of free will as an element that transforms the universe from mere mechanistic laws to a process of consciousness.

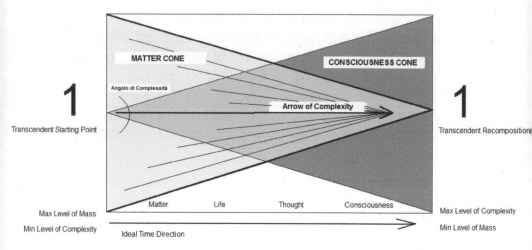

In fact, what was first sustained by the laws, results as then being subject to progress, to power and therefore to human choice. It evolves in proportion to awareness and to the capacity to make itself interpreted by the nature of things, progressively on all levels, beyond those that are local, temporal and material.

Therefore 'added value' is not just simple progress, seen as an automatic optimization of the functions of the system, even though that process up to a certain point functions per se, but an added value that re-enters the field of the emotions, feelings, sensitivity. A spirituality that is seen as the capacity to *give significance to things*. One that goes – and leads us – beyond those same things, to take us back to eternal values. The 'significance' is proportional to our capacity to perceive and to interpret: it is the awareness that gives value to Form. It is really this spiritual result that sustains the entire universe and that transforms it into an open system and therefore a dynamic one.

All worlds and dimensions share in the complexity of the universe each one producing a different aspect of the whole result. If a dimensional plane does not produce 'its' result it will be synchronically dissolved in laws, or destroyed and reconfigured: the universe is structured according to the criterion of saving. Looking back over the epochs, according to stellar and galactic clocks, complexity is the rhythm that beats the time of evolutionary currents but also the moments in which the universe – if we can say so – 'takes stock'.

This could be a key to reading the universal flood and the epochal changes that distinguish the terrestrial and universal eras. It is interesting to note that the myth of the 'universal flood' is often interpreted as a natural consequence of 'degeneration'.

Whatever it is, all Form in the diversity of its experience tends to go in this common direction. Form inclines towards the infinitesimal (less mass) and towards multiplicity (more relationships). It diversifies towards relational systems which are more optimized and complex, able to sustain information, memories, experiences, higher and transcendent functions and thus produce complexity. It is a substantial but 'subtle' result: it does not relate to Form as such, but the relationship between Form, the perceptions, intelligence and the total significance that every system expresses. It is the interaction and elaboration of the transformation.

Scientifically,

According to the theory of the 'growing arrow of complexity', the universe had its beginnings in a very simple state, basically a ball of almost uniform energy which has now become very differentiated and complex. Life in general and human beings in particular are glaring examples of this tendency. Here there is no contradiction with the second law of thermodynamics, because living beings are not isolated systems, in fact they are systems that are defined as 'dissipative', dependent on an uninterrupted interaction with their environment for their continuity. We can maintain our notable order thanks to the entropy that we yield to and which surrounds us, for example when we breathe out carbon dioxide as a waste product of our metabolism[55].

Subtle, psychic and spiritual motors exist that sustain this infinite motion, nourished by *awareness*: the expansive force of the spirit.
In fact, through its mechanisms of perception and interpretation, it extracts significance from every single thing until it reaches a total sense of the reality. We are talking about a holistic result (the total is superior to the simple sum of its parts), including an added value that sustains the universe itself, justifying the manifestation as expressions of the Absolute Being capable of 'consciousness'.

Complexity is therefore a result of the relationships between Form. However it is not merely a mechanistic process or automatic and natural but becomes *potential* when it depends on the exercise of intelligence. Complexity increases proceeding from the past to the future but this is no longer automatic. Given the nature of the laws, complexity increases when Form

---

[55] Extract from *The Time of Man and Time of God*, intervention by John Polkinghorne, physicist and Anglican Priest, member of the Royal Society, illustrious President of Queens College, Cambridge, made in the cycle of conferences Scientific Paths, *The Faces of Time*, organized by the Milan Cultural Centre.

comes into play at a level which activates the functions of *free will*, evolution is then subject to the dynamics of awareness and therefore to choice. This is the path by which divinity makes up the real nature of this universal field: our universe becomes increasingly the 'right' field of choice, operated in part by a growing consciousness rather than selected by a mere mechanism of laws. Spirituality is therefore an extraordinary act.

The production of added value is a process which is based on emotion and in the ultimate analysis on *Love*. In terms of physics such spiritual awareness could be likened to 'weak nuclear forces' which perhaps correspond to *"that one unique force, Love, that unites infinite worlds and renders them alive"* (Giordano Bruno). In fact while electromagnetism would appear to constitute the frame work of our illusory material reality and our conventional space-time, it is the weak interaction that animates the emotional and spiritual processes that truly keep the universe cohesive and sustain it as a field of consciousness.

It is possible to refer to renewed models of reality if we use our senses and a new kind of logic; deep down we are playing with illusions: whether one or another thing is true really does not matter. What matters is where that one or other thing takes us. We live only in the suggestion we decide to create. *Thought creates*, always and everywhere.

The equilibrium in the relationship between time and complexity considered on the basis of our standard, generates the electromagnetic field that creates our plane of three-dimensional existence made of mass-energy-space-time, just as we understand it and just as our science understands it.

281

If complexity increases at the same rate, the relationship is recalibrated by different standards and gravity could also be influenced by it[56].

This is what could possibly happen with the advent of a New Era of awareness.

Such a phenomenon on a planetary level could appear as an acceleration of time, increasingly perceptible also on the human plane.

The increase in complexity/consciousness due to an evolutionary acceleration deriving from elements of awareness and free will, would re-configure temporal and spatial relationships and allow us to determine a more 'elevated' reality.

Consequently, in order to obstruct an increase in potential complexity (or consciousness) resulting in the reformulation of concepts of humanity and reality, one would have to make time 'denser', that is, maximize the saturation of events or 'import them' by correspondence, or as a result of gravitational effects (for example of planetary mass) so as to compensate for the increase in relative complexity and therefore re-establish and conserve the current equilibrium between time and complexity: the electromagnetic or gravitational cage that imprisons us.

---

[56] An effect that perhaps was once obtained in a local form by means of technological solutions for making mass
'lighter', as many daring archeologists or academics seek to demonstrate with regards to, for example, the construction of the pyramids on the part of antediluvian civilizations (another example could be made with certain meditation techniques which would produce anti-gravitational effects for exactly the same reason: the alteration of the relationship complexity/time).

NO 2 forces.

Kabbalistic Correspondences

The following interpretation of the terms used in the Tree of Life highlight the possible correspondences between Esoteric Physics terms and the traditional Sephiroth, distinguishing what happens beyond the Abyss of successive manifestations.

MACROCOSM	
Ain	Nothingness
Ain Soph	Infinite Time
Ain Soph Aour	Infinite Energy
Zureh	Humankind Primeval Divinity
Rashit Ha Gilgolim	Primeval Laws
Nekudah Rishovah	Primeval Laws Meeting-Point
Sephiroth Habinyon	Derivative Laws
MICROCOSM	
Guph	Physical Body
Nepesh	Instinct, Environment, Education
Ruach	Soul Personalities/Center of Mass
Chiah	Free Will
Yechidah	Divine Spark
Neschamah	Attractor/Real

Taking another look at the dynamics of creation described in the first chapter, we have seen that from Nothingness (*Ain*) the infinite, made of infinitely non-manifested potential (*Ain Soph*) springs a paradox: the meeting between Void and Time, from which an infinite energy arises (*Ain Soph Aour*).

This energy is modulated through a geometry: it receives a direction and therefore structures the necessary conditions for universal manifestation. From the 'concept of universe' (*Kether*) issues the world of ideas (from which the archetypes of the worlds originate) and the world of numbers (from which originate the archetypes of events): Binah and Chokmah. even
uneven

That process is renewed at different levels of the creation in all its phases. From these 'primordial spheres' reflections are generated on the dimensions in a successive scale – on the mental, astral, etheric and spiritual planes – to endlessly manifest on multiple planes of *elemental* and material existence (*Malkuth*).

Nothingness *Ain*

Infinite Time *Ain Soph*

Infinite Energy *Ain Soph Aour*

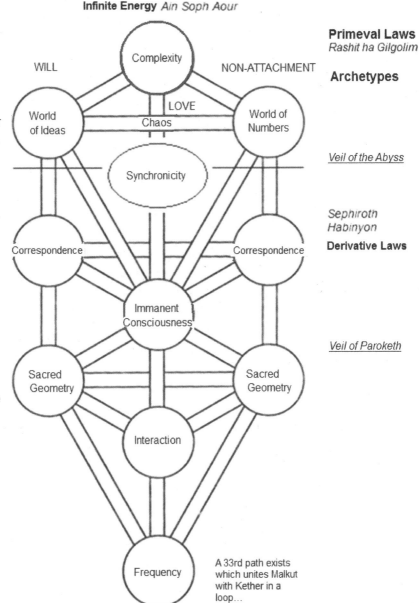

Primordial Point
Jekudah Rishovah

the evolution from matter life, thought and onsciousness is related the 4 worlds of reation (assiah, etzirah, briah, atziltuh) nd to the formula of the ETRAGRAMMATON /HVH) and its Elements.

a wider sense the rmula of the ETRAGRAMMATON cludes all the rocesses:
OD – anomalous wave E- meeting point AU – multiplicity E – re-composition

onsciousness Shekhinah) develops in uch a way as to achieve e spiritualization of natter: YHShVH (the ENTAGRAMMATON) - e symbol of an/Humankind.

WILL

Complexity

NON-ATTACHMENT

LOVE

World of Ideas

Chaos

World of Numbers

Synchronicity

Correspondence

Correspondence

Immanent Consciousness

Sacred Geometry

Sacred Geometry

Interaction

Frequency

Primeval Laws
Rashit ha Gilgolim

Archetypes

Veil of the Abyss

Sephiroth Habinyon
Derivative Laws

Veil of Paroketh

A 33rd path exists which unites Malkut with Kether in a loop…

285

Appendix II

Notes on the Esoteric Concept of Time

Time is the moving image of eternity

Plato

It is now understood that time is not just a sort of passive and immutable container of events and Form. Instead esotericism considers time as a real and *natural kingdom*, living and intelligent, which is in symbiosis with all the other manifestations of being - dimensional, spatial, material and living - of which time itself is a support and fundamental constituent. Where space exists, where Form manifests and has room for continuous transformation and reciprocal interaction, time is perceived – and in effect operates – as a *sequence of events*.

Outside of space and the *material* dimensions the concept of the *flow of time* has no reason to exist and its functioning mechanisms are of another order. Once investigated they enable us to understand its real nature much better.

Time is the first effect of the meeting of primordial forces from which the universe springs: the first result of the creative act, when the universe is still distinct from the All as a virtual manifestation of the Absolute Being. The development of universal manifestation into existential eco-systems and living percipients triggers the beginning of the 'flow' or of a *mental* sense of reading in which cause and effect structure the temporal link from one event to another. This is necessary for measuring and giving significance to Form, its transformation and reciprocal interaction at every level.

With the advent of quantum physics, modern physics has begun to investigate the infinite relationships that are woven by Form and time: relationships in which cause and effect no longer recognize one another through interconnection.

As the evolutionary direction of our universe is one of complexity, in theory, past times correspond to less complex systems, while future times correspond to more complex system. A structure in which the universe consists of an ever increasing diversity of mass able to express functionality or support information/memory on a wider scale inside a scheme that is increasingly evolved. I say in theory, because of the combination of joint causes already analyzed, linked to the expression of consciousness and free will and because it could happen, that time (the plane of Form) develops in a totally different manner in respect to the direction of complexity. Furthermore the events, seen as the possible relationships between Form, do not 'fall' on the axis of the flow of time in a uniform way, instead they are more intense in correspondence to lines where there is an increased probability of complexity manifesting: for example the Synchronic Lines. What's more they arrange themselves inside a precise temporal sequence that we define as 'time packets', that last on average 70 years.

As the human being is the point of convergence of many natures, from that of the material, to that of the soul, the divine and the spiritual, depending on where it positions the barycentre of its identity – in a way more pertinent to the material illusion or more in the direction of its higher nature – it can interact differently with reality, space and time. Sometimes it is more or less willingly bound by material existence, at others emancipated from any kind of restriction.

Time Travel

From an esoteric point of view time travel is a practice which, although not that common, is (or has been) experimented with by many different schools and traditions. This extraordinary experience is not to be confused with simple time prospecting but regards the possibility of moving and acting in time, just as if the latter were a territory, a navigable ocean, a sort of circuit on which an infinite number of connections can be created.

'Time packets' contain events/Form saturated to a level of use that is proportionate to the complexity they participate in. Temporal movement is based precisely on that margin of complexity which allows a more evolved being to re-saturate events at a higher level of use, bringing the historical reality of the principle plane back into discussion. The being (the 'temponaut') moves around the fabric of reality to redefine it, aligned to the particular rhythm of the 'time packets' which allow him to slip inside events 'in counter time' and re-saturate them acting as a higher complexity.

The alternative reality that is obtained develops on an echo of the principal plane. The echo world can, in different ways interfere with the principal plane itself, even though it is far away from it, or impose itself as the principal plane by substituting the previous one (which would mean that it had never existed).

According to esoteric theories that explore time travel as a physical phenomenon, there is no movement of mass but only of 'information': if necessary the information required for the physical constitution of the *temponaut* is used to reassemble his body - though not with the same atoms that had composed the original - but rather by reorganizing the atoms and particles that belong to the destination site.

In current thinking time travel should be part of a broader approach to research, one that investigates laws and dynamics rather than just the material world and the universe: an investigation into the human mind and its power to manifest and determine the reality that it perceives.

As Time is a 'territory' we could imagine true and proper wars being waged for its conquest and control, thus the development of nations or 'temporal' empires rather than spatial ones that correspond to the control of certain epochs or temporal sequences, even on a sporadic and non-continuous level. In this context the concept of 'alien interference' would without doubt acquire an even more fascinating dimension.

Even though it might appear an event of pure science fiction or even *hyper- science*, according to various sources, typical of the panorama of contactees of the 1980's, among whom can be found Carla Rueckert (*The Ra Material*) and Ashayana Deane (*The Freedom Teachings*), we are all living in a relative present: we are actually on an alternative existential plane that is progressively substituting the original plane that has already been lived! On the original plane earthly humans reached a point of no return as far as surviving on the planet was concerned. However, certain astronomical dynamics, special operations and 'outside help' has generated a new *existential wave* (which we could liken to the concept of the Age of

289

Aquarius of Eon of Horus/Maat) that could promote an evolutionary thrust towards a different outcome through a greater evolution of consciousness. It is hypothesized that certain terrestrial and alien forces that have already controlled (and control) this planet for many millennia are interested in maintaining humanity in a state of slavery. They are working to safeguard humanity and the planet in order to safeguard their supplies of food-life-energy. For now it would appear they have managed to create an alternative plane of events (that which we find ourselves on) to preserve humanity, saving it from probable extinction but aimed at maintaining its subjugation on a genetic, psychic and spiritual level.

Wot about " Many Worlds ?

In fact through repeated exercises that were concluded with the empire, the war and the divisions, you have been obstructed and hit by those who have taken possession of the power and the command of your sphere, to the point in which your entire planetary sphere has been moved from the normal flow of time/space into what this instrument (Carla) calls a lateral time. It is a sort of diversion in which a train can be moved from the main track until it has been repaired.

interestly idea
NWO as g rint ?.

Q'uo through Carla L. Rueckert[57]

y flawed

---

[57] During the 1980's, after many years of research and intense group meditation, Carla Rueckert began to enter into continuative telepathic contact in a trance state; at first with a friend who had recently died and then with an 'extraterrestrial entity'. This new path of research of the ' L/L Research' began on the 15[Th] of January 1981, and proceeded for a total number of sittings amounting to 50 until 1982. The sittings were monitored by Don Elkins and transcribed by James McCarty: those transcriptions (taken from audio recordings) were collected to form the so called 'Book of Ra' or 'Ra Material'.

Over and above the metaphors and the mythical–poetic images, this is a representation of the individual crossroads between consciousness and unconsciousness, responsibility and indolence, realization and bewilderment.

The Human as a 'Temporal Being'

Your consciousness is faceted to express light into multiple systems of existence. There are many, many expressions that comprise your total Selfhood, and each expression is linked to the hub of consciousness that is your core identity. It is here that your ancient voice and eyes can multi-dimensionally observe, express, and experience. This is your food source for expansion and beautification. Place your attention upon your core identity and never release it. With every piece of information that passes your way, discern how it enables you to attune to this voice and perception. This is the only discipline you require. It is the remedy of limitation.

The Wingmakers – an excerpt from Memory Activation

Knowledge of our own *lives* does not correspond to an exercise in memory but to the fact that a level of consciousness is reached which allows us to perceive them, in as much as they are being lived, conscious of the contemporaneousness of our diversified participation in time and in our different 'incarnations'.

Proceeding with this vision of our being, we could consider ourselves first and foremost as *temporal beings*, endowed with attractors and divine sparks, in which our incarnations and their *fruits*, the

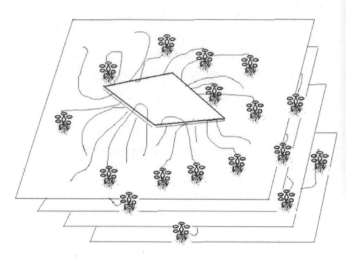

matured personalities in formation, are rooted in material structures. The bridge is constituted by this macro-being which 'draws out' of the world of Form, by means of its roots in it, life blood (complexity, added value), made up of experiences and significance which through our ramifications nourish our divine immanent and in the ultimate analysis, transcendent being. The diagram below illustrates the many strata of space and time that represent all the possible dimensions of complexity and consciousness in which our 'complete body' is distributed.

above

Mysterious Archaeology

With the term *'Mysterious Archaeology'* we mean the investigation of the past aimed at the profound, one that sets out to restore the barycentre of reality in ourselves and, in this case, of history.

From the point of view of anthropological and archaeological investigation we can summarize by bearing in mind the following precepts.

1. We know very little about our very distant past
2. Our origins our much more ancient and mysterious than what we were taught at school
3. Darwinism is not sufficient: Creationism and Evolutionism have to find new links and meeting   points
4. Perhaps our origin is not terrestrial or not only terrestrial or simply, we need a different logic to consider and understand our genesis, our ancestors and our history
5. Certain 'extra' interference from outside or from the depths - or from a ufological and spiritual point of view – should certainly be considered, also through the interpretation of Mythical figures.

Today we talk about archaeology, pyramids, stars and mysteries of the past, of important proof and discoveries, alternative interpretations, ancient and mysterious civilizations: they are all very fantastic and stimulating but what conclusions do they arrive at?

The interest that they inspire expresses the need for a new awareness, new logic and new answers and questions.

A fresh approach is needed to know and understand reality, through which the human being can recover full control of its own faculties and existence. An approach through which it can interact with the 'supernatural' and with all possible dimensions of reality.

However, even though it is true that, "He who does not know his own past, has no future", we cannot afford to stop paying attention to the present - of which we have but a distant perception. We need to come to terms with the fact that the key to understanding the past, the present and the future is to be found inside of us.

The truth is not 'out there' but 'in here'!

The Author

For over twenty years in parallel to his profession as a management trainer and company manager, Carlo Dorofatti (Milan, 1970) has been involved in different fields of free research: including meditation, traditional medicine, metaphysics applied to avant-garde psychology, spiritual traditions, modern frontier disciplines and investigations into new existential models of well-being and awareness. He holds conferences and seminars in Centres and Institutes all over Italy and abroad.

Founder of the *Centro Studi Ascensione 93*, from 2008 he has been a member of the *International Conference on Ancient Studies* – together with Graham Hancock, Robert Bauval, Michael Cremo, Robert Schoch, Andrew Collins and other important international exponents of free and independent research. He writes for many specialist magazines and online portals and his first book *Nient'altro che se stessi –Incanti e disincanti della Nuova Era* was published by Nexus Edizioni in 2010. He currently lives in Vigevano (PV), Italy.

Website: www.carlodorofatti.com

From the same Author:

CARLO DOROFATTI
Nothing but Oneself
Enchantment and Disenchantment in the New Era

This interesting and original essay lucidly analyses many of the aspects that characterize the New Era announced so long ago by spiritualists and prophets of all continents which has led to an authentic fervour in the last decade. This book pitilessly lays bare the deception and dangerous psychological conditioning that threatens to deviate the individual from the real aim of this noble and important event.

Turning concepts that have become dogma on their heads and illustrating the authentic significance of terms such as 'initiation', 'illumination' and 'ascension', this book is a precious aid in discriminating between the many sources available for those seeking to truly understand and realize their role in a rapidly advancing New Era.